BITTER OR BETTER

YOUR CHOICES AFTER DIVORCE

Electronic and soft-cover print versions published by
the Wellness Institute,Inc.
1007 Whitney Avenue, Gretna, LA 70056

Cover design by the Wellness Institute, Inc.

***SelfHelpBooks.com** is a division of the*
Wellness Institute, Inc.
Gretna, LA 70056

ISBN: 1587411105.

Printed In the United States of America

BITTER OR BETTER

YOUR CHOICES AFTER DIVORCE

By

Deborah K. Leporowski, Psy.D.

This book is dedicated to my husband, Tim, without whom this project would not have been possible.

ACKNOWLEDGMENTS

I am indebted to every single individual who uttered the words "you should write a book" to me over the past ten years. In particular, I am thankful to the many veterans I was privileged to know at both the Miami VA Medical Center and the West Palm Beach VA Medical Center – it would not be appropriate to name you all and I fear I would accidentally omit a name, but you know who you are. Thank you for trusting me enough to share your life stories and for encouraging me. I admire all of you.

A heartfelt thanks goes to my friend, Dr. Patricia Ferguson, who provided long-distance emotional and editorial support and stopped to read the final manuscript in one night for me.

To my ongoing clients, thank you for your understanding during this project and for constantly reinforcing to me that people do get *better*.

I am truly blessed to have two friends who never faltered in their belief in me and this project – thank you, Deb and Marianne.

I must thank Dr. Harold Dawley at Wellness Institute for believing in an unknown author.

I am grateful to my children, Emily, Patrick, and Kyle who endured repeatedly hearing "I'm working on my book" – somehow, we found enough time for everything!

And finally, and most importantly, I am grateful for my husband and genuine partner, Tim, for his patience, unwavering encouragement and loving support. What an amazing cheerleader you are!

TABLE OF CONTENTS

INTRODUCTION

So. You've decided to read about life after divorce. If you purchased this book yourself, congratulations! I sincerely hope this means you are open to making thoughtful, new decisions about your life. Perhaps someone gave you this book and you're not really sure you need it or want it. In any event, if you're going through the divorce process or you've recently divorced, or even if your divorce was finalized quite some time ago, you may be feeling alone. But you can't really be alone, because it's still true that the divorce rate in this country continues to be extraordinarily high with at least fifty percent of all marriages in the United States ending in divorce. Twenty percent of Americans will divorce twice! Despite the best efforts by the mental health profession, this phenomenon leaves millions of Americans struggling with the aftermath of divorce.

In my work as a clinical psychologist, I have found that while many people survive the actual process of their divorce, many are so profoundly affected by this event that they fail to make a successful adjustment in their life post-divorce. Many individuals are stuck in bitterness, anger, and resentment. I went through a divorce myself, and found myself faced with an opportunity to choose to view my divorce as the catalyst for significant change in my life.

I invite you to ask yourself what you think about divorced people. You may not have thought of this before, but you've been receiving messages about divorce your entire life. Deep down inside, do you think of people who are divorced as failures? If being married was a very important part of your identity, you may find yourself feeling like a failure.

I suspect you are going to be surprised when I ask you to start thinking about your divorce as an opportunity – a crisis that provides the perfect opportunity to re-examine virtually all aspects of your life: the kind of work you do, where you live, how you manage your finances, how you manage your emotions, who you surround yourself with, how you approach new relationships, managing the inevitable challenges of raising children after your divorce, your health and appearance, even your faith and how you want to practice it.

The list of possible reasons why your marriage is ending or ended is probably infinite – infidelity of one or both partners, "incompatibility", religious reasons, constant arguing, you "grew apart", one of you wanted children and the other one didn't, an addiction that wasn't addressed, your sexual relationship was lousy, there was emotional or physical abuse, etc. This book does not address what already happened. If you came to me for therapy after your divorce, you'd hear me say to you "now what are you going to do about it?" This book presumes that the event has already occurred, and I am going to insist that you learn from your marriage that has ended and accept responsibility for your role, but the focus is on making healthy, conscious choices about many facets of your life *today.*

I am going to insist that you face facts. If I can get you to face facts, your divorce can be the catalyst for tremendous, meaningful change. I want you to explore who you really are without your former spouse and to take personal responsibility for your own happiness. Reading this book will require you to embrace the fact that your choices produce consequences in all areas of your life. There is really no room for making excuses.

Many people could benefit from seeking the services of a psychotherapist to deal with the ending of a marriage. Admittedly, individual psychotherapy is expensive, and many people are reluctant to engage in a therapy relationship. My goal in writing this book was to provide a private, very economical way to assist divorced individuals in accepting responsibility and making deliberate, superior life choices.

Recovery from your divorce isn't going to happen overnight. But it will happen when you decide to make a conscious choice about how you want to be – *bitter or better.*

The farther behind I leave the past,
the closer I am to forging my own character.

Isabelle Eberhardt

Chapter 1

The Opportunity in the Obstacle

"If you are willing to learn and grow, you can use disaster to enrich your life."

Bernie S. Siegel, M.D.

Could your divorce be the catalyst for some new kind of independence? An opportunity for significant changes in your life? As both a clinical psychologist and someone who has been through a divorce, I understand that it probably doesn't feel like it at first, but what if you made a choice to view it that way? Has it ever occurred to you that without having gone through a divorce, you might never have had an opportunity to explore your own resourcefulness? How interesting that the written Chinese characters for "crisis" and "opportunity" are the same.

Think for a moment of how young children are often resistant to new experiences and will generally continue to rely on adults unless forced to go out on their own at various points in their development. For example, the very first time a child has an opportunity to spend the night at a friend's house, although they may be filled with excitement about the invitation, they are typically simultaneously also somewhat anxious and afraid about being away from home. Most children really don't want you to take the training wheels off of their bike – they don't trust themselves enough to ride the bike without assistance and they assume they will fall and become injured. I have found in my clinical work that it's really not that much different with adults and how they feel about new experiences.

Consider how many times you have experienced something that seemed awful at the time but ended up providing a tremendous life lesson. How many times have you heard of what first seemed to be the *worst* thing happening to someone that turned out to be the *best* thing sometime later? Where have your thoughts been focused during your divorce and how are they influencing your decisions and where those decisions will lead you? Be careful about what you are telling yourself.

Perhaps you have been reinforcing to yourself a variety of beliefs about divorce that you aren't even consciously aware of. Most people are reluctant to admit that they talk to themselves, but we all do. Maybe not out loud, but we always provide ourselves with a subconscious running commentary.

For example, have any of the following thoughts crossed your mind? Do you wonder if there is something wrong with you because your marriage ended in divorce? Do you think God is punishing you? Have you considered yourself stupid because you picked the "wrong" person? Have you told yourself that divorce is wrong and you really ought to reconcile with your former spouse at any cost? Have you been told that divorce was "unheard of" in your family of origin? Do you feel as if your life is over? Do you believe that you'll never be happy again? Do you worry about what others will think of you? Have you privately devalued the institution of marriage itself? You will need to explore these thoughts in depth.

I have noticed over the years that working with people who are surviving a divorce is often quite similar to working with patients who are trying to survive a very serious illness. You may have even noticed that you felt that way at times throughout your own divorce process, as if you were just getting over the flu. There is tremendous loss involved in a serious illness as well as in a divorce – loss of a major relationship or of a partner, loss of a body part, loss of function.

In both situations, people feel as if they are being forced to give up a part of themselves. How you deal with giving up a part of yourself has a great deal to do with how you defined yourself *before* the loss, and even more significantly, how your future will ultimately unfold. You will be changed, of course, but you are still you. You are still you, minus a husband or wife. You are still you, minus the house you used to live in. You are still you even when your children are spending the weekend with their other parent. You are still you, minus a gallbladder, or a breast, or if your hair falls out. So why does this feel so threatening?

I suspect it's because there is significant emotional pain involved. People are often annoyed when I remind them that pain truly is a necessary part of life, that uncomfortable and unpleasant symptoms are necessary. Pain is intended to get our attention! Pain is a necessary part of divorce just like it is a necessary part of an illness. Pain is designed to alert you that *something is not right.* Pain is not totally escapable.

In fact, the total absence of pain isn't necessarily all that desirable. Without pain or discomfort or some kind of alteration in your body's functioning, how would you know when you are ill and needed to get medical attention? Pain is designed to get you to pay attention and take care of yourself or to seek help. Pain is also instrumental in helping you to avoid further injury. When you do something incorrectly and it hurts you physically, clear-headed rational people tend to avoid doing it again.

The same is true of emotional distress. When you interact with others in a dysfunctional relationship, it doesn't feel good, and logically you would want to avoid future interactions of the same quality. Emotional distress, especially when not dealt with or repressed, often produces physical symptoms like an illness. Those symptoms are valuable and serve an important purpose.

I haven't yet met anyone who has gone through a divorce, even the most amicable divorce, and not experienced it as a significant, painful event. Divorce can seem like a very lonely experience – particularly in the beginning, it feels as if you are the only one who has felt that kind of pain. This is particularly amazing in light of the fact that almost *twenty million* people in the United States have been through a divorce!

Despite this fact, you may be consumed by the feeling that no one really understands what you have gone through. The first thing you wrestle with after your divorce may be your own identity. Suddenly, everything seems to be in transition and things seem to be uncontrollably happening *to you.*

Consider this - what if you harnessed the power of that event of your divorce to transform your life by paying closer attention to your real intentions, desires, values, talents, and interests? Believe it or not, that's what some seriously ill patients have done who have survived life-threatening illnesses and who will tell you that their illness or disease was a *gift*.

So, now that you find you aren't a part of that old relationship anymore, isn't it likely that you need to find out who you really are apart from that relationship? It may sound trite, but you probably need to rediscover *you*. And if you really aren't sure who you are, this is the perfect opportunity to ask yourself *now that I'm divorced, how do I want to be?* What have you done so far in this process of growing through your divorce? My hope is that when you have finished this book, you will be motivated to develop a much clearer picture of how you want to be and will begin to act like the person you want to be even before you put into action all the choices you decide to implement.

So, one aspect of the opportunity in the obstacle is that, if you are willing and interested, you receive the gift of getting to learn more about *you*. Your divorce can provide an opportunity for you to become more self-reliant and, for some of you who need this, to gain skills in assertiveness as well. Your divorce may be the first time you have ever really looked at your life and realized you have been on auto-pilot despite the fact that you have always had choices about how you live your life. You have already unconsciously defined what your priorities were by where you invested your time, energy, and money.

Think about it for a moment – you can tell what someone's priorities are by where they invest their time, energy, and money. For example, you can insist all you want that watching television isn't important to you, but if that's how you spend hours of your life, night after night, you've obviously allowed it to become a priority with your investment of time. Likewise, you can determine what is *not* a priority by the absence of the time investment.

If a lot of your energy went into your marriage or emotionally supporting your former spouse, does that priority make sense now? Having more knowledge about yourself means that you can use that information to successfully develop the kind of life that will meet your needs and fulfill your heart's desires. Without that knowledge, you're likely to just mimic what makes someone else happy – and that choice will produce results that won't be fulfilling for you.

Let's look at some ways in which you could find out more about who you are now that you are no longer married. There are undoubtedly some activities that you might have always wanted to explore but never got around to for one reason or another. *Now* just might be the perfect time. Marriages need to have an element of healthy compromise, however, many divorced or divorcing people complain bitterly about the compromises they made during their marriage, typically blaming their former partner.

When you were married, you may have relinquished certain interests or activities as part of that compromising. Are there interests or activities you would like to rediscover? Take a moment to think of what they might be.

One newly divorced woman I know did something as simple, yet liberating, as taking belly-dancing classes! It was an activity she had always secretly wanted to explore but had never done so before because her former husband had ridiculed her. Now, as a single woman, she was thoroughly enjoying herself one night a week as she got more physically fit and made new friends.

Another woman returned to church following her

divorce. In her case, it wasn't necessarily to fulfill a spiritual need or to turn to religion in a crisis as so many people do. She had been married for many years to someone who was Jewish. She was raised as a Catholic. They had raised their children in neither religion, almost ignoring major holidays. Although she had not originally viewed this as a sacrifice while married, when her marriage ended, she felt that it was time to revisit that aspect of her life and to make a conscious decision about whether to actively practice the faith in which she was raised.

She initially returned to the church where she had last been a member, but it had been many years and she did not feel welcomed. Consequently, she visited other nearby Catholic churches and even made appointments to discuss her situation and concerns with a few priests. She continued her search until she eventually found a church "home" where she could begin to actively explore her religious background and to regularly practice her faith in a way that was meaningful to her.

I have witnessed many individuals return to pursuing a college education only after going through a divorce. Often, it had not been a priority in the marriage because their partner had not viewed it as a priority. Could this apply to your situation?

Part of compromising in a marriage can involve making concessions on issues that you previously felt strongly about. Now is the perfect time to revisit some of those issues and to decide which issues are no longer negotiable in your new life, areas where you now know you cannot compromise. Make a list of those areas that apply to you.

Don't overlook another important way in which you can find out who you really are – learning to say no to requests that encourage you to be who you really *are not.* As you look for the opportunity in the obstacle, many of you may have to practice becoming more genuine and must get over your fear of *not* doing something. Just going along with everyone else's interests and priorities is not part of the route to becoming *better.*

Learning to say no is a lot more difficult for some of you than it is for others. Do you find yourself agreeing to things that don't feel like they are compatible with who you are or who you want to be? If you know you tend to be a "people-pleaser", this may be difficult for you to change. You may simply agree with requests in order to avoid conflict. If you can learn to say no now, you can avoid feeling frustrated and unhappy in the future.

I'm not suggesting that you say no indiscriminately just for the sake of it, but that you take a moment in each situation to examine whether saying yes would truly fit in with your priorities at this point in your life as you are striving to become better after your divorce. Does it really make sense to commit to all of the same activities you did when you were married?

Take a moment right now to think about something you would love to say no to if it were guaranteed that you wouldn't suffer any negative consequences. Is there a commitment you made that you'd like to break if there were absolutely no repercussions? I'm not asking you to arbitrarily avoid honoring your commitments.

I'm asking you to think about those areas of your life where you would like to say no if you weren't saying yes just to avoid your fears about what others might say about you or think of you. When you become more aware of when you should say no, you begin to develop a more authentic lifestyle for yourself without lingering resentments.

But what if your idea of the opportunity in the obstacle

is that someone will come along and *fix* you and make you happy? I want to be very clear about this: **if you need fixing, it's your responsibility**. You can't afford to wait around for someone to heal you from your divorce. People who are willing to rely on someone else for their happiness are routinely disappointed. You know the old line about not waiting for your ship to come in but swimming out to meet it? Well, I'm going to ask you to take action and swim out to accept responsibility for your life and embrace all the new possibilities that can occur. The choices we make as individuals determine the consequences of our life. What do *you* need to do to fix you?

Many years ago, a young woman was referred to me for psychotherapy by the local community mental health center. She had been abused or neglected for practically her entire life. She had almost no possessions that she could call her own and typically lived with someone who would take her in. She was dependent upon others for almost everything. She was quite disabled by her anxiety and depression and at the time I was seeing her, she was not employed and had no marketable skills. She had not even finished high school.

She would often mention in our therapy sessions that all she wanted was "the house with the white picket fence", and we would explore what that meant to her. Unfortunately, for quite some time, she made no deliberate efforts to change her circumstances but just seemed content to complain about her lot in life and to allow others to control her.

One day, as she once again mentioned "the house with the white picket fence", she suddenly had a realization that was marvelous to observe and the kind that provides the joy in my profession. She told me that it had just occurred to her that perhaps instead of waiting for what she wished for, she needed to go out and buy the lumber, build the picket fence, and paint it white herself!

So, how do you go about finding the opportunity in this obstacle of divorce? What is the first step? The first step is **acceptance**. Acceptance of your current situation means acknowledging that your marriage has ended, it does not mean accepting your fate as a divorced person as others might define it.

Let me clarify what acceptance *is not.* Acceptance is not denial. Acceptance is not hopeless resignation about your fate. Acceptance is not avoiding the inevitable reality. Acceptance is not behaving like what you think other people expect a divorced person to behave like. Acceptance is absolutely not portraying yourself as a victim. This may seem ridiculously obvious, but without acceptance, you simply cannot become empowered to make life decisions. You must come to terms with the fact that your marriage has ended in order to address your future as a single person.

Unfortunately, I have encountered too many people who refuse to accept that their marriage had ended. Once it is over, *why* it is over really becomes irrelevant except where your behavior may have contributed. One woman I know continuously filed numerous, immaterial lawsuits against her former husband *years* after their divorce had been finalized, challenging almost every decision that had occurred throughout the divorce process, even filing a lawsuit which sought to have the final judgment of the divorce itself overturned! Sadly, and not surprisingly, her life did not move forward at all but was characterized by isolation, vindictiveness, and anger – traits which her children could readily see and which diminished her children's respect for her.

I want you to remember an important principle as you are going through this difficult time – **growth occurs in the valleys of life, not on the mountain tops.** Think about it for a moment and you'll recognize that it's true. Look back on the other frustrations and challenges of your life prior to your divorce. Throughout your life, you most likely didn't do very much significant growing when things were easy, routine, and calm. You stretched and strained and grew when things were most challenging.

Growth occurred during very painful, honest discussions with someone close to you or when you were faced with some kind of test of your ability and you were uncertain you would come out on the other side. Growth occurs when you are awaiting test results. Growth doesn't occur when you are feeling on top of things; growth occurs after you survive your darkest hours. I assure you that you will grow from this experience in a positive way if you choose to do so.

But what if you are someone who views your entire marriage as a mistake? Its easy to slip into the stance of "but I wasted twenty years of my life!" I hear those comments quite often. It probably wasn't a mistake, but even if you choose to see your marriage that way now, that's okay, because mistakes are *always* opportunities. In fact, that's all they are, unless you choose to not learn from them and repeat them.

Unless you deny the mistake or make excuses for it, mistakes are opportunities to learn from experience and to acknowledge our faults. I would caution those of you who are comfortable viewing your marriage as just one big mistake that you are taking a very global, impressionistic, uncritical stance about what actually went wrong and consequently you are going to miss opportunities to learn about yourself that you can apply in future relationships.

Another thing you must do is to examine all of the possibly distorted beliefs about marriage you have brought with you through your divorce. For example, beliefs such as "all men (or all women) are jerks" or "women (or men) can't be trusted", "I'll just lose myself if I get married", "there aren't really any good marriages", etc. The problem with these beliefs is that some time ago in the process of your marriage, you decided they were absolutely true and therefore don't need to be tested. I think we've all met someone who insists (post-divorce) that all members of the opposite sex are simply rotten and can't be trusted, so they'll "never get married again".

Well, I just always have an association to lemons when I hear that – not the fruit, but the word we've come to use to describe a car that had an inordinate number of mechanical problems. I'm sure you have either known someone or heard of someone who purchased a "lemon" or maybe it happened to you personally.

What I want to know is this: have you ever known someone who bought a "lemon" and then because of that *one experience*, lived so in fear of getting another "lemon" that they never owned a car ever again and walked everywhere? I doubt it. So why would an otherwise reasonably intelligent person stick to a distorted belief and choose to rule out a relationship with any one of *millions* of people on this planet on the basis of *one* failed relationship?

Its normal to feel vulnerable – but not for ten or more years! I've listened to numerous people who have been divorced for eight, fifteen, even thirty years and they had made themselves into an impenetrable island. They certainly were successful in making sure that no one hurt them in an intimate relationship again.

The only problem with this stance is, and its a *huge* problem, they stayed focused on their pain all of those many years, justifying to themselves their bitterness and resentment and closing themselves off to any opportunities to relate and connect with people who could help them in the healing process. Their strategy for responding to such a difficult event is to construct their lives in such a way that they ensure that they will never trust or love again.

Feeling so vulnerable tends to have a strong relationship to *blaming* your former spouse for what went wrong in the marriage and your willingness to stay in the victim role. You may not want to hear this, but part of what I will ask you to do is to confront *yourself* about what really transpired in your previous marriage. No matter what the original causes of your divorce were, this period of time can be a time of tremendous transformation for you...if you *choose* to make it so.

In addition, sometimes divorced people are reluctant to develop even nonromantic friendships. This phenomenon isn't always related to difficulty trusting others, or fear of getting another "lemon". Often, it's a reflection of your damaged self-image following a divorce. Without even realizing it, you may be behaving as if you are damaged in some way. Do you secretly feel no one would really want to be in a relationship with you? After a divorce, you may be feeling "unlovable", and this can extend even into your friendships. You can end up wearing your divorce like a handicap of some sort. So, what you think you deserve is what you will get.

Another unfortunate way I have seen this damaged self-image manifest itself is through promiscuous sexual behavior immediately following a divorce. For some of you who are feeling particularly insecure about yourselves, this may be an area where you feel you need to prove something.

Many divorced people allow themselves to be motivated unconsciously by the painful reminder that the person with whom they were in an intimate, committed relationship ultimately rejected them sexually. Your sexual relationship in your previous marriage may be specifically where you feel the most wounded and inadequate.

Unfortunately, dangerous, casual sexual activity at this stage typically reflects a strong undercurrent of unaddressed anger and self-loathing. It may seem easier for some of you to develop a pattern of promiscuity than to deal with your fears about real intimacy. You're feeling lonely, hurt, and not necessarily all that attractive. Consequently, while frantically trying to prove your sexual attractiveness and ability to seduce others, you are increasingly likely to increase your own level of vulnerability and to get hurt in the process.

Sleeping around with various people can also be a common avoidance tactic so that you don't have to spend any time alone with your feelings. You may make excuses that this is all you can handle at this point – you don't want any intense emotions or commitments. You should be aware though, that chronic promiscuity can be indicative of significant depression and anger, and of course can now involve potentially life-threatening risk.

If this is behavior you're engaging in, you'll need to ask yourself why and what it is that you're avoiding. Fortunately, most people don't remain too long in this phase and move on to more mature sexual involvements. Re-evaluating your sexual behavior is another potential opportunity that comes from the obstacle of divorce, so use it as one. Getting stuck here though, will definitely prevent you from becoming *better*.

Chapter 2

Managing All Those Feelings

"A man is happy so long as he chooses to be happy and nothing can stop him."

Alexander Solzhenitsyn

For most people, going through a divorce is a bit of an emotional roller coaster ride. There may be no other time when you can simultaneously experience such a variety of mixed emotions. One minute you're relieved to have that jerk out of your life, and the next minute you're feeling panic-stricken about how you are going to survive financially. It felt really good to hang that picture up on the wall in your home exactly where you wanted it, but then you remembered that event you've been invited to tonight where everyone will be part of a couple but you.

At the end of all those feelings is a goal of acceptance – being content wherever you are. Not complacency, but being content where you are in the process while motivated to get to where you want to be. In the middle, however, you'll likely experience fear, shame, anger, sadness, resentment, bitterness, denial, emotional exhaustion, loneliness, vulnerability, and sometimes a little exhilaration.

Perhaps feeling overwhelmed by a variety of emotions is what prompted you to read this book. Let me assure you that this transition time is always characterized by a myriad of *feelings*. Some of you may recognize that you've been swinging back and forth between anger and depression.

One of the influences that made this book into a reality was my ongoing awareness both from reactions of others to my own divorce and from clinical work with patients that there seemed to be a consistent *perception* about divorce - that this particular life event carried a powerful, pervasive, and usually perpetually negative connotation regardless of the particular circumstances.

Somehow, expectations developed in our culture that have dictated how we should respond to such an event, how we should view ourselves if we had gone through the process of divorce, and how we should view others who are divorced. I don't really know how this happened with an all-too-common event such as divorce, but as a psychologist, I have discovered that the truth is that each one of us can individually choose how we will react to the event.

We can choose the *meaningfulness* of the event. You can even choose to alter your feelings. My personal choice, and the philosophy that I have tried to impart to those I have been fortunate to work with, has been to accept divorce, learn from it, and use it as an opportunity to become even *better*.

Even though the experience of divorce is, in fact, a very common crisis with well over one million divorces granted each year in the United States, leaving at least two million divorced people, it *feels like* a lonely, solitary experience. Why then is it that some people seem to fare better than others after their divorce? (And why does it seem at times like everyone else is faring better than you?)

In my clinical experience, it generally all boils down to how you choose to perceive the impact of the divorce – do you recall my comments in the previous chapter about people who are struggling with a life-threatening illness? Perhaps you may not have thought of it this way before, but you have viewed your own divorce through your own personal (possibly distorted) lens that tells you how you will perceive many events.

Some people, when challenged, find that their thoughts automatically move toward an analysis of "what am I supposed to learn from this?" This is very much different from thinking "why me?" "What am I supposed to learn from this" represents an attitude of embracing that there is always a lesson to be learned from change – often painful lessons, and that a crisis represents an opportunity for growth. Unfortunately, this attitude is one we may aspire to but which doesn't come all that naturally to most people. All too often, we become easily consumed by the *feelings* we have surrounding an event, which can prevent us from dealing effectively with the reality-based aspects of the event itself.

The most common reaction for the majority of people following their divorce appears to be *fear*. You've undoubtedly experienced some of it yourself just as I did, and you may still be experiencing it at times. That feeling of fear (or anxiety or worry) can be related to numerous aspects of your life.

For some, it is a fear that is very much focused on finances and the financial changes that have occurred as a result of the divorce. For many, it is a very fundamental fear of being alone. Some men and women, particularly those who married young and were married for many years and have never been on their own before, naturally feel somewhat frightened because it is a previously unknown experience. You may have a fear of dating and interacting with new people. Perhaps you are experiencing fear about whether anyone else will ever find you attractive again. Perhaps you are afraid of what others will think of you now that you are divorced. Will others judge you as defective in some way?

I remember that one of the fears that arose in my life shortly after my divorce was a trivial, unexpected one that I had not anticipated. My children were fairly young, and I had decided to drive from south Florida to North Carolina with them during their spring break to visit with my parents. I had made many long car trips with my ex-husband, driving for as much as twenty-four hours straight through to our destination by taking turns driving.

However, about a day or two before I was to leave for North Carolina, I suddenly realized that I had never driven for more than about five hours by myself, let alone for twelve or thirteen hours with three kids in the car. I must tell you that I felt intimidated and not all that enthusiastic about the prospect of doing all that driving by myself. I wasn't confident that I could do it, and I began to think of all the possible things that could go wrong.

Now, you may think that this is a pretty silly experience to be afraid of. And you're right – in retrospect it does seem rather silly. But the point is that I had simply not done it before, so I didn't know that I could be successful. The only way to conquer the fear was to face it for what it was and make myself become enthusiastic about the trip, plan for it as well as I could, portray it as an adventure to my kids, and just do it!

So, of course, we went, the trip was uneventful, my kids and my parents were proud of me, and best of all, I felt a great sense of accomplishment. The reality is that without being forced to do so because of the circumstances of my divorce, I might never have known that particular feeling of accomplishment. The next time I decided to jump in the car and take a trip with the kids, it was no big deal.

Many fears are totally unfounded – such as my fear of driving a long distance alone with my children. I really had no justifiable reason for feeling afraid – I just allowed myself to feel that way because it was "uncharted territory". The fear went away when I confronted it with my actions.

You might want to take a few minutes to list all of the fears you have now that you are divorced. They don't have to be life-threatening fears, and you don't have to reveal them to anyone else. But I do want you to acknowledge them and come up with a plan for confronting them.

For example, perhaps you are a woman who has never bought a car on her own before and now that you are no longer married, you find that you need to do so. A lot of people are intimidated by the negotiations involved to purchase a car simply due to lack of experience. That might be a fear that goes on your list. Or perhaps your fear is about a bigger purchase – buying a house or condominium on your own for the first time. I recall that it certainly wasn't at the top of my list of fun things to do! The only cure for your fear is to do the relevant homework and then *do it!* Sometimes, the best advice a therapist can give is to tell you to just *do it afraid*.

Marriages (ideally) involve compromise and shared responsibilities, so it's likely that there were some tasks in the marriage that your spouse typically handled and with which you are inexperienced. You might be afraid of approaching those tasks. For example, some of you have never prepared and filed your income tax return by yourself. Well, that's okay - now it's your turn! Just because you don't have a spouse now doesn't mean that you can't ask someone else for assistance if you need it. Asking for assistance in a particular area does not identify you as incompetent – it demonstrates your desire and willingness to learn. Don't forget that our President has numerous advisors!

It is quite likely that deep down inside you are afraid that no one will love you or find you attractive. Probably the most powerful fear we have as humans is that we will be rejected. If this is a common fear for most people, it isn't too surprising then, is it, that these feelings would surface on the heels of your divorce. You may be experiencing that very scary, wake-up-in-the-middle-of-the-night-with-your-heart-pounding, kind of panicky, existential fear that you will be all alone with no one to care for you when you are eighty-five years old.

Of course things are going to be a bit scary at this point following the break-up of your marriage. If you look back honestly on your life, you can easily recall many times when you naturally experienced fear but you had to move forward anyway – I'll bet you even felt afraid on the first day that you went to high school!

If your family moved when you were a child, you probably experienced a fear of fitting in and making new friends every time you arrived at your new location. I'm certain that you have felt the fear and anxiety of starting a new job. For you women with children who are reading this, you very likely experienced fear when you found yourself in labor and about to give birth.

You must confront your fears unless you are content

to live your life on the sidelines. I caution you to avoid using fear as the excuse for not getting on with your life now that you are divorced. This *is not* the time to withdraw because you are afraid. Don't allow yourself to become lonely and isolated. Giving in to fear will sabotage your efforts to become the *better* person that you truly want to be. Although fear sounds like a very negative term, it can become a very comfortable excuse – avoidance of new experiences and settling for what you already know is easier than confrontation.

It might seem to you at this point in your life that you can solve some of these problems related to your divorce through avoidance – and temporarily, I suppose you could. You may be feeling desperately afraid of rejection if your former spouse is the one who initiated the divorce, and you are determined that you are just *not* going to set yourself up for rejection again. So you could choose to avoid interacting with people as much as possible. However, if you give in to your fears now, you are going to get stuck. You may initiate a subtle pattern of fear-based avoidance. You are going to get stuck because you are making assumptions about what will happen in the future based on fear that is rooted in the past.

Often, people who have gone through a divorce actually feel ashamed of their divorced status. Understandably, this phenomenon seems to be more common if you did not initiate the divorce and felt it was somewhat out of your control. You can feel as if you were blindsided. Suddenly, everyone is expressing how they feel *sorry* for you. Although their intentions are good, all of that sympathy can allow you to feel even more entitled to feel bad and tends to reinforce your avoidance.

I am aware that there are some books out there that make distinctions about your ability to grow after divorce based on whether you were "dumped" or "left" versus whether you were the "dumper" or the one who left. I don't believe these distinctions are generally relevant. When a marriage fails for any reason, it is stressful and it just doesn't *feel* good. The critical issue is to ensure that you do not turn the failure of *the marriage* into your personal failure, which is unfortunately exactly what I've witnessed in many of the divorcing patients who have come to me for help.

Are you one of those people who have experienced moments of feeling like a "loser" since your divorce? Have you been aware of feeling pitied because you are divorced? You know, sometimes people even expect you to act like more of an emotional wreck than you are at the time!

I distinctly remember when I was going through my divorce and was in the process of feeling somewhat stronger, I ran into someone who actually said to me "why aren't you crying?" She had an expectation that I should be behaving as if I was falling apart. Well, I had already done my share of crying, and I just wasn't at the point anymore where crying seemed to make much sense.

You may have felt that people are somehow avoiding you since your divorce – and your perceptions may be quite accurate. Unfortunately, people often don't know what is appropriate to say to you in these circumstances, so they say nothing. Most of us have had the experience of running into someone that has recently had a death in their family and wrestling with what's appropriate to say – sometimes we aren't sure whether they would like us to acknowledge the loss or not. It's difficult to know whether to bring up a painful topic. It's also possible that what you have experienced may be frightening to some people who have some serious doubts about their own marriage or realize that their marriage is in jeopardy. Divorce *is not* contagious, but you'll likely encounter someone who acts as if it is! You may find yourself feeling uncomfortable with your single status and consequently declining social invitations.

It is quite common to feel a sense of disconnection with the rest of the world as you go through your divorce and are re-entering the single life. You can feel as if you are chronically on the outside looking in at everyone else's seemingly well-put-together life. It's that sensation of feeling lonely while you're in a crowd. This disconnectedness can leave you feeling vulnerable, and so while you are painfully aware of feeling disconnected and needy of others' attention, you may be pulling back into yourself to protect yourself. The challenge is to try to balance self-protection with your human need to be connected with others.

Let's talk about that really intimidating emotion – anger. First, let me assure you that some anger is okay early in the divorce process, even necessary. I am always concerned when working with someone who vehemently denies experiencing even a trace of anger. Certainly, anger is to be expected when we feel we have failed at something, when we feel betrayed, or at the loss of a dream.

However, some of you have experienced or may still be experiencing really debilitating, intense, unhealthy levels of anger. In my clinical experience, I have found that intense anger during or continuing after the divorce is usually most likely related to unresolved negative feelings during the marriage that were not acknowledged and rarely or never got expressed.

This may come as a surprise to some of you, but prolonged anger is rarely helpful or productive. If the event or person that you believe is provoking you to anger is someone or something outside of your control (and it usually is), you are allowing some external event to control your emotions. Do you feel entitled to be angry?

Well, in fact, there is no law against continuing your feelings of anger. The real issue here is whether your continued anger will benefit you in any way or give you any advantage in life. I can tell you from my clinical experience what chronic anger is most likely to do for you – it will keep you feeling frustrated, it will tend to drive people away from you, it will steal your joy because you can't be angry and happy at the same time, you will feel trapped by your emotions, and you will be much less likely to achieve your goals.

But did you know that you can *choose* how you feel about your former spouse, even when you feel entitled to angry feelings? Let me give you an example of how controlling your feelings about your former spouse rather than letting them control you can be life-changing and how this actually worked for a woman I know who went through a very difficult divorce involving betrayal.

Carol, as I will call her, was understandably devastated when her husband of about fifteen years walked out on Christmas Day and left their family to be with another woman. Frankly, she was in shock. They had two great, intelligent children together and had been high school sweethearts. She had lived in the same relatively small town all of her life and knew many people. It quickly became apparent that this extramarital affair had been going on for some time and was not a secret in the community, and Carol became consumed by embarrassment, shame, and then by anger. I recall her telling me about her fantasies of all the awful things she wished would happen to her husband to pay him back for the pain and embarrassment she felt.

A few months went by with Carol feeling furious, bitter, and resentful every day. Her children took on these feelings as well and wanted nothing to do with their father. Carol cried a lot and began to develop many physical symptoms as well – migraine headaches, joint pain, and weight loss. Her doctor prescribed tranquilizers, and she began to feel increasingly dependent upon them. It was impossible to have a conversation with her that did not include a reminder of something awful her husband had done and her subsequent plan for retaliation.

One day, she announced to me that she had made a conscious decision to do something different that she hoped would help to curtail her anger, as she could begin to see that her feelings of bitterness towards her now ex-husband were consuming her daily life. What did she do? She decided that no matter how hard it might be, she would pray for her ex-husband every day. She reasoned that she could not genuinely pray for him while simultaneously experiencing hatred towards him. I remember how she emphasized to me that the power in this approach lay partly in the fact that he would not be aware of what she was doing and so could not stop her from engaging in that activity.

The results were dramatic. Soon, his name did not even come up in a conversation. Carol started to feel better physically and began to look better. She returned to church and joined a singles group for divorced people at her church. She obtained the financing for a new business. Her children seemed to take their cue from their mother and began to interact with their father more frequently and in a healthier manner. She stopped expressing her resistance to her children visiting with their father.

And as she let go of her anger and resentment, she was able to allow new people into her life – she no longer projected the image of what she had, in fact, been – an angry, bitter victim. She even got to the place where she could understand, accept, and forgive her ex-husband's deceitful behavior during the latter part of their marriage.

Now for those of you reading this who are thinking to yourself "well, I could never do that," remember, it's a choice. If you say you could never do it, you're right, you probably won't. And its not easy, but please remember that how you choose to treat your former spouse has a great deal to do with whether you'll be *bitter or better.*

Some of you who are reading this book are wrestling with emotions that are in response to feeling betrayed. That betrayal may take the form of a basic betrayal of the marital commitment to remain together if your former spouse initiated the divorce.

You may feel betrayed if your spouse chose to end the marriage when you were committed to remaining married at any cost solely because that is what you believe you vowed to do.

The betrayal may involve specific behaviors that occurred during the marriage wherein your spouse had an affair and the very intimate nature of the marriage was not honored. Consequently, you lost respect for one another, and this may have led you to feel like you cannot trust members of the opposite sex.

The majority of us were raised to understand and respect that marriage is a sacred covenant, the most intimate human covenant with the fundamental principle of faithfulness. Understandably then, any violation of this covenant often results in tremendous mental anguish for the betrayed party.

If your spouse was unfaithful and you have suffered

betrayal in your marriage, I sincerely regret that you endured such a hurtful experience. It is truly unfortunate, and it would be wonderful if human beings treated each other better.

Despite this, I want you to be very clear about a few points. What has already transpired is done – you cannot change it. The reality is that there is no turning back, and it cannot be undone. It will not help you to dwell on it. It will not help you to try to assign blame – to yourself or your former spouse. And most importantly, it makes absolutely no sense to add to the hurt that you have already experienced by remaining hurt or resentful any longer than is absolutely necessary for your healing and allowing that hurt to evolve into something more destructive and enduring.

Feelings of betrayal over time can most certainly lead to profound bitterness. If you were betrayed in the covenant of marriage, what you have been through may be characterized as a bitter experience. However, if you embody that bitterness and view the entire world through a distorted lens of distrust and bitterness where every event is seen in light of your hurt, you are choosing to become a bitter human being who will live a *bitter* life.

Although you may project the emotions that you are carrying around inside of you to the outside world, anger, bitterness, and resentment have a remarkable way of only affecting *you* – not the person you have targeted with these feelings. But here is something you also need to remember - *your body is the only one* that is really the repository for all of the physiological reactions that go along with those feelings. Think about it – the target of your anger and resentment doesn't necessarily even have an awareness of how you are feeling, but you have the potential for the migraine headaches, the ulcer, the high blood pressure, the sleep disorder, the shortness of breath, the heart palpitations, the grinding teeth and the TMJ symptoms.

This is not simply my opinion – this is scientific fact! When you are chronically angry, bitter, and upset, your body remains in a chronically stressed state of arousal that is *physiologically* damaging – and totally contradictory to a state of physical health and emotional peace and wellness. When Carol began to consciously pray for her ex-husband, she altered her physiological state and could not maintain anger and bitterness along with a spiritual state of peace.

The famous cardiologist Dr. Herbert Benson coined the term "Relaxation Response" while at Harvard Medical School in the 1970's as he studied how the human body responded to practices like praying, meditation, and progressive relaxation. Importantly, he found that our bodies do not discriminate between Christian prayer, Buddhist prayer, transcendental meditation, hypnosis, progressive relaxation, or biofeedback. The "Relaxation Response" refers to the resulting lowered blood pressure, heart rate, and respiration rate and need for less oxygen – responses that are incompatible with anger, bitterness, and resentment.

So, now many of you may be saying "but I'm entitled to feel this way, I didn't deserve this." Well, perhaps you're right, you probably didn't deserve it. What I hear most frequently is an acknowledgment of these feelings accompanied by "but I can't help it!" Oh, but you *can* help it. I have yet to work with or encounter an angry, resentful individual who isn't absolutely certain that their feelings are justified.

Somehow, if we feel we are "right", we think these feelings are okay to hold onto. But there's no reward – you just get to be bitter, angry, resentful, *and* right.

If you are one of the people I'm referring to who is chronically carrying around these miserable, resentful emotions, you know who you are. This is probably the most critical point of the entire book, and it doesn't have to be specific to the experience of having gone through a divorce.

We can easily find plenty of reasons to feel slighted, hurt, or angry – there are no shortages of these opportunities in life. In fact, not a day goes by where we aren't given an opportunity to feel slighted or offended by someone if we choose to do so. But, if you *know* that you carry anger, hatred, bitterness, hurt, and/or resentment in your heart, please read this chapter as many times as you have to until you are certain that you understand these principles, as painful as acknowledging your responsibility in the process may be at this time.

You cannot convince me that you can somehow build the healthy life you claim you want based on being wholly justified in your ongoing anger about a set of circumstances or towards someone who hurt you. It will not work. In fact, you'll probably get sick and eventually die in the process. There is nothing sadder to me, as a psychologist, than to watch someone choose to remain in the bondage of anger and resentment, losing the person they once were or hoped to be.

So what can you do about those feelings? First, you must accept that you have been choosing to let a painful, open wound travel along with you everywhere you go. In every human interaction, there's that open wound, never healing and constantly influencing your behavior. Note that I said *you have been choosing.*

This means that it is likely that you consciously think about who or what has hurt you *over and over again.* Perhaps you even play some particularly painful dialogue that occurred with your ex over and over again in your head, repeatedly cringing at the hurtful words that were said to you. You are not helpless over your own thoughts – they are yours, no one else's, so therefore you choose them and they are your responsibility.

You probably simply haven't made a significant effort yet to replace your angry, hurt, or victimized thoughts with forgiving thoughts that could free you. I can't possibly know what transgressions have been committed against those of you reading these words right now. But I do know from working with hundreds of individuals that *forgiveness* is the key to becoming *better*.

You are a human being with flaws, and you were married to a human being with flaws. You do not have the same flaws, but nevertheless, neither of you are perfect. You apparently thought at one time that your former spouse had some redeeming qualities when you married him or her. Likewise, they must have had the same thoughts about you. Did you make mistakes for which it is impossible to be forgiven? So are you really in any position to refuse to forgive?

When you look at someone who is angry and bitter and unwilling to forgive, you can see it all over their face and in their body language. You can tell that they are clinging to something, even if you can't see what it is. When you refuse to forgive, you permanently alter who you are to incorporate the negative emotions. That altered *you,* your bitter and angry self, consequently interacts with everyone else on a daily basis who *hasn't* hurt you and doesn't deserve your anger in a manner which doesn't allow you to fully give of yourself – what emanates from you is tainted by your unwillingness to forgive.

You don't just take your anger and bitterness out occasionally when you think it's useful and conceal it the rest of the time. You might think this is how it works, but let me assure you that it doesn't work that way. Instead, your anger and bitterness leaks out everywhere, in sarcasm, caustic remarks, fear, ambivalence, passive-aggressive behavior, uncooperativeness, distrust, and pessimism. When you encounter something wonderful, you contaminate it with the germ of your internal anger which originated from something or someone totally unrelated.

When working on this issue with a client in a therapy relationship, which is all too frequent, the key is to enable the individual to understand that the forgiveness issue is about *them*, not the person who hurt or abused them. Forgiving frees *you*, not the other person, although sometimes they may seek your forgiveness. Forgiveness is empowering. Whether your former spouse is "sorry" or not is really not the issue at hand. This may be hard to accept at first, but it doesn't matter at all. The real issue is whether you want to break out from your self-imposed emotional prison.

Related to this issue, I'd like to share with you the emotional area which I believe can be one of the most damaging and most reinforcing of remaining bitter and not getting on with your own life – overinvestment in your former spouse's life. By that, I mean a*re you obsessed with your former spouse*? Consider these questions which will help you identify whether you have been able to let go of the past and whether your preoccupation with your former spouse's life has reached obsessional proportions.

- Do you think about your former spouse daily?

- When you are home alone, do you wonder what your ex is doing?
- Do you pump your children for information about their other parent's activities?
- Do you talk about your former spouse frequently?
- Do you try to arrange to be in places where your ex is likely to show up?
- Do you frequently feel the urge to contact your ex when you have nothing else to do?
- Do you harbor any fantasies of revenge to wards your former spouse?
- Do you have jealous feelings about your former spouse – about where they went on a vacation, activities they had with the kids, about a recent achievement, the kind of car they drive, where they live?
- Do you call your former spouse frequently and unnecessarily?
- Do you demand information from your ex that is really none of your business?
- Do you ask friends, neighbors, or relatives of your former spouse for information?

If you answered yes to even a few of these questions,

you are *way too involved* with your former spouse's life. Look where you are expending a lot of your energy – on someone who is no longer married to you. You aren't taking charge of your life; you are being a spectator in your ex-husband or ex-wife's life!

Your thoughts indicate what you are interested and invested in, and if your thoughts are constantly about your former spouse's activities, interests, relationships, employment, etc., you are living in the past in a former relationship. Your excessive thoughts about your former spouse are creating very real consequences. This kind of preoccupation is probably not allowing you to be a very pleasant, enjoyable, vibrant person to be around right now.

If you are so preoccupied, or obsessed, with your ex-husband or ex-wife, it tells me that you are choosing to live in a reactive stance to someone else's life, probably as a victim. If you are spending time thinking about where your former spouse is going on vacation, what does this say about your vacation plans, or lack thereof? If you are obsessing about where your former spouse lives, are you dissatisfied with where you live but doing absolutely nothing about it? Are you seething about that new car your ex is driving? If you are obsessed with your former spouse's social life, what commentary does this provide about what's going on with *your* social life? Do you see my point?

If this discussion of preoccupation applies to you, your current emotional problem is not about your former spouse's life, it's more likely that you haven't yet built your own life! The source of your difficulty isn't in your former spouse's life, it's in yours.

I'm sure many of you are feeling that my words are overly blunt right now, but they are the absolute truth.

Remember, you need to face facts if you are to become *better.* If this obsession with your ex doesn't feel very good (and I know it doesn't) and isn't getting you what you want in your life now that you are divorced, then you are going to have to acknowledge that you've been allowing your thoughts and behaviors to linger in that area and make a conscious decision to do some things differently.

Don't expect your former spouse to change their behavior in a way that will give you less to obsess about – its ridiculous to expect that your ex will stop taking vacations so that you'll no longer be jealous about them! Just because you are hurting inside as a result of your divorce and are focusing too much on your former spouse's behavior and activities, this doesn't mean that they are to blame for how you feel. You are accountable for your thoughts and feelings. So what can you do about it? How can you pull back from this obsessional style?

Well, not surprisingly, you'll have to acknowledge that you have a problem in this area rather than justify it – you have to label your obsession for exactly what it is. Without truthfully acknowledging that you are obsessed with your ex, without taking ownership of these thoughts and consequent behaviors, you can't change it. In fact, by denying it, you are likely to get even more entrenched in this behavior, practically guaranteeing that you'll remain *bitter.*

The next step is to identify what has been maintaining or reinforcing your behavior – for example, what happens when you try to get information out of your former spouse that is none of your business? Do you feel like you need the interaction? Do you somehow relish finding out negative information? Do you get to recreate some kind of familiar explosive interaction between the two of you?

This is not random behavior. If you are preoccupied with your former spouse's life and engage in these types of activities, on some level you perceive that there is a pay-off of some kind, some kind of outcome that is reinforcing to you (no matter how dysfunctional and self-destructive).

Whenever you find yourself reaching for the phone, "grilling" your children about their other parent's activities, talking to your friends about your former spouse's latest escapades, or starting to ask others about your ex, stop and think about what you could do *in that moment* to focus on *your* life and making it *better*.

And finally, lets examine feeling depressed after a divorce. First, let me clarify that depression is not the same emotion as sadness or grief. As a psychologist, I don't diagnose depression in the immediate aftermath of someone suffering a loss. Those feelings are viewed as normal grieving, and only after they last for months are they viewed as something out of the ordinary, a depressive disorder.

Some sadness is to be expected. You may need some time to mourn the loss of how you viewed an ideal marriage. Your plans for your future have changed. You can't envision your retirement with that individual any more. You may have assumed when you got married that it would simply last forever. Perhaps a committed relationship takes more work than you were previously aware of investing. Sadness is legitimate and not impacted by our personal distortions in the way that a depression involves serious distortions in our thinking.

A lot of "finger-pointing" goes on during a divorce. By this, I mean the big and small accusations that are lodged against each party. Painful as this may be to hear, there's often a small grain of truth in some of these accusations.

As you mourn the loss of a marriage, don't ignore the information about you that is embedded in the accusations. Accepting the truth about ourselves as it was displayed in the marriage, whether it be an acknowledgment of failing to continue to take care of our personal appearance, not dealing with a bad temper, falling short on responsibilities, not dealing with an addiction, or just being "unavailable", cannot be denied and must be faced if we are to become *better*.

When you made a conscious decision to read this book, you took an active step against ongoing heartache, grief, or becoming depressed. However, if the people who are closest to you have voiced concern about how you are doing and have expressed worry about your mood or appearance or you feel that perhaps you are suffering from a clinical depression, please consult with your physician or a licensed psychotherapist. If you are crying daily, feeling worthless and/or hopeless, are experiencing thoughts of suicide, are eating excessively or not at all, or are sleeping excessively or very little, you need to seek the help of a professional as soon as possible.

If you feel you are experiencing some depressive symptoms which are less severe than those I listed above, I would recommend that you thoroughly examine your thoughts. You will find that your thoughts probably contain many distortions. Take a look at what you are specifically telling yourself about the situation of your particular divorce. For example, you may be telling yourself that you will never get over this, that you need a partner in order to survive, or that you cannot be happy alone and therefore you are depressed. These are exaggerations - a distortion.

One quick way to challenge your distorted belief that you cannot be happy alone is to make a list of enjoyable things to do alone, activities that don't require another person such as writing a letter or an e-mail to a friend, going to an art museum, reading a book, going jogging, watching a video, playing with a pet, or taking a class so that you can learn something new. Challenge your assumption that you can't enjoy yourself alone.

Likewise, if you are relying on using drugs or alcohol in an attempt to manage your feelings, you need to seek the help of a professional immediately.

So what is my advice to you about how to manage these negative, destructive emotions? Well, first you must accept that some of them simply initially come with the territory – they are to be expected during this transitional period, but they are *temporary*. This is particularly true with respect to feeling lonely and an inability to be alone. The goal is to make sure that they are temporary so that you don't get stuck in them.

After you accept that you are going to experience a variety of emotions, **get inspired by something bigger than yourself.** What do I mean by this? Get involved, become passionate about something unrelated to yourself, do something different, invest your energy outside of yourself, just break up this pattern of being self-absorbed and self-involved! How you specifically choose to do this doesn't matter other than reflecting your basic interests. What matters it that you step outside of your own life, your own temporary misery and turmoil, even if just for an hour or two. Doing so will break the pattern of your negative thoughts and feelings and start you on your way to becoming *better.*

Do something for someone else that is totally unrelated to the experience of going through your divorce. Volunteer – some organization needs you! It doesn't have to be complicated. Let me give you a simple, yet effective, example.

Several years ago, I was working with a young woman who was very depressed over the abrupt break-up of her relationship. She was so upset that she found it difficult to go to work each day, and her job was in jeopardy due to the days she had missed and her tendency to burst into tears while at work. She lived by herself and had no children, and she found herself aimlessly getting through the days, obsessing about her ex, eating too little and sleeping too much. Fortunately, she was a tremendous animal-lover and found some comfort in her two dogs, cat, and a horse, and she had always enjoyed occasionally stopping at an animal shelter to look at the animals.

One day, she stopped at the local animal shelter on her way home from work to look at the dogs and suddenly had a simple, but powerful idea. She decided to stop there regularly, once a week, to pet each of the dogs. She realized that most people viewed the large dogs in the cages but do not make contact with them as they do with the puppies unless it is a dog they are considering adopting, and yet they all need physical contact. She began to look forward to her weekly visits to the animal shelter and would be happy when she found a dog had been adopted since her last visit. The shelter staff looked forward to her visits and complimented her on her contribution to the shelter.

These brief, weekly visits to the animal shelter provided her with the much-needed break from her obsessional thoughts about the loss of her relationship and got her focused on the needs of animals – something she already felt strongly about.

Another effective way to change the current negative pattern you may find yourself wallowing in is to **consciously alter your thoughts to focus on gratitude.**

In other, old-fashioned words, *count your blessings.* Every single person you know has been wounded by life events in some way. Because you are reading this book, I know that one of your particular wounding events is your divorce. But your divorce certainly isn't all there is to your life. Don't let one event overshadow all that you have to be thankful for. What are you grateful for despite your divorce?

If you are feeling really despondent about your divorce right now, you might be saying to yourself "I don't have anything to be grateful for". However, this simply cannot be true. If you spend just a few minutes each day reviewing what you currently have rather than reviewing the marriage you lost, you'll be able to better manage all those feelings.

You are reading this book, so one of your blessings must be the ability to read – don't take it for granted; many Americans are illiterate. You either had the money to buy this book and access to a bookstore or to the internet to order this book, you have access to a library, or you had someone who cared enough about you to loan or give you this book. They sound like blessings to me, but perhaps you just never stopped and thought to look at it that way.

You are probably reading this with a roof over your head and a bed to sleep in tonight – more blessings many people in this country wish they had. You woke up this morning and had the opportunity of another day. Many people did not.

Gratitude journals have become somewhat popular in the last several years, and I've used the practice myself and endorse it to some of my patients when I feel that it would be helpful. At face value, a gratitude journal might seem overly simplistic, but I believe there is some subtle, hidden power in seeing in print what you personally are grateful for, day after day.

You might want to start small – just get a little notebook, journal, or notepad and begin the day by listing what you are grateful for. Three to five entries is good, but if this feels uncomfortable to you, why not start with just one entry every morning? Don't be too hasty; spend a few minutes contemplating what you are grateful for. It doesn't have to be earth shattering, just genuine.

Perhaps you are grateful for something you might have previously taken for granted, like acknowledging a friend who is available and willing to listen to you when you are feeling insecure. You can be grateful for having a job even if you don't particularly like the job that you have at the present time. Perhaps it is simply gratitude for a spontaneous hug from your child. What better time to focus on counting your existing blessings than during a time that appears to be a crisis. Don't forget to celebrate the small stuff – it all counts.

Chapter 3

Taking Responsibility For Yourself

"Shallow men believe in luck. Strong men believe in cause and effect."

Ralph Waldo Emerson

If you haven't deliberately done so already, you must begin to take charge of your life. The reality is that you don't get to turn to a supervisor or boss to dictate how you should take responsibility for your own life. In my opinion, right now is the best opportunity to take responsibility for yourself and the only life you have been given. How well are you doing with this assignment?

Ask yourself this question: Would someone else hire you to be in charge of *their* life based on your current performance as the boss of your life? Here's another way of looking at it: If someone accused you of being in charge of your life and therefore responsible for the outcome, would there be enough evidence to convict you? If not, you've got some serious work to do.

You are the one who gets to design your life's plan, and for some of you who may have been in a dependent stance in a very controlling marriage, this may be new and a bit scary. In my clinical experience, I have found that during and immediately following the divorce itself, many people often fall into an insidious, passive course of self-neglect. I am continually amazed at the ways in which people will abandon taking care of themselves following a divorce such as simply not going to the dentist even though they might have done it regularly when they were married. I know there is no rule about neglecting the care of your teeth because you're divorced – you aren't divorced from your dentist!

Most of the people I have worked with simply weren't even getting a reasonable amount of sleep or eating properly and were surprised that they feel awful. Are you one of those people who are getting through the day by living on caffeine? It seems like such an impossible task to try to take care of yourself when you are overwhelmed and going through probably the most stressful experience of your life, but it really is fundamentally important. Do you need to pay more attention to your health and/or appearance?

I have found that many people equate taking care of themselves with being "selfish", especially divorced mothers with young children. Taking care of your health and appearance is not synonymous with selfish, but I'm going to ask you to prioritize your life and be selfish anyway. If you are a single parent with young children at home, there are numerous demands placed on you, and you can't very effectively take care of your children's needs through a plan of neglecting your own. You can't be there for the people who are closest to you, either physically or emotionally, if you are running on empty.

It might seem to work at first, but eventually it will break down as you become exhausted, angry, resentful, and physically ill. You can delay addressing this issue for quite awhile – usually until there is an emotional or health crisis. I want to alert you to the need to make some changes before you are forced to do so in a crisis. What's required here is *balance.*

All living beings are endowed with some capability for homeostasis, and all the systems of your human body have mechanisms for homeostasis. The true nature of our lives is that there will be constant change – to deny that and insist on treating our lives as static experiences will only cause us intense frustration.

But what does this mean for your current situation, the very reason you are reading this book – the fact that you are going through or have gone through a divorce? What you knew in your marriage may have represented a "comfort zone" of sorts – even if your marriage itself was *very uncomfortable.* If you stop to think about it and are very honest with yourself, even the uncomfortable parts probably had some predictability to them.

Often, staying in that uncomfortable "comfort zone" is indicative that you may have a problem with dependence and feeling that you cannot exist outside of the security of a formal relationship. Remaining in your old comfort zone actually makes this journey through your recovery from divorce more difficult than it has to be and inhibits you from taking charge of your life. Now that you aren't married, it is expected that you would initially be feeling somewhat out of your "comfort zone".

During or right after a divorce is a particularly common time for many people to express that they feel trapped, without alternatives. In my experience, when someone comes into my office and tells me that they are "trapped", what this really translates into is that they *believe* they have no *choices*. However, when we explore this, they inevitably find that, in fact, they absolutely do have choices, but the choices are often very difficult ones. Do you confuse difficult choices with no choices?

Think about it this way – if I tell myself that I have no choice in a matter, that I'm simply trapped, then there really isn't anything for me to take responsibility or action for, is there? I can just quit right there. (Oh, and I get another opportunity to be a victim, too.) You may have to look long and hard to see the choices, but they are always there.

You may tend to conveniently overlook the options that are very painful ones. Sometimes, the only choice we seem to have is how we *choose* to perceive our situation. But that's enough to make a difference. Now is the time to focus on what you *can do*, not what is outside of your control.

Let me give you an example of a divorced patient of mine whom I will call Lynn and how she came to realize she wasn't trapped and chose to become more responsible for herself after her divorce. Lynn had been married for about 17 years and had three teenaged children. When she came to see me, she had already done quite a good job of coming to terms emotionally with the reasons why her marriage had failed.

She wasn't particularly angry or resentful, and she had a clear, reasonable view of her ex-husband. Lynn's divorce agreement included a large, one-time cash settlement for Lynn with monthly child support for the three children. Of note, part of their particular agreement was that she would maintain the responsibility for providing health insurance for herself and the children.

Lynn expressed that she was mostly dissatisfied with

her own life since her divorce. Lynn did not have a college education, nor did she really have any marketable skills. Her family had not been supportive or encouraging about education, and she had really never thought of obtaining a college education as an option.

Lynn had been a stay-at-home mom throughout most of her marriage and then had obtained a job as a cashier at a grocery store when her children were a bit older. She disliked her job intensely and didn't like her coworkers either. Unfortunately, after her divorce, she had lost some friends and the only friendships she had were at the store. Often, she got assigned to shifts that she didn't like. She was convinced that her only skills were as a cashier.

At first glance, this looks like a simple case of job dissatisfaction. However, it was really much more serious because Lynn had been spending the original cash settlement from the divorce quite freely. In fact, in a little over a year, she had spent most of it. It was clear to me that she was living way beyond her means with little regard for her future.

Lynn felt trapped in a number of ways. She had been renting an expensive house after her divorce, which was using up a lot of her money. She was moving backwards financially. She couldn't see any alternatives on her own. She felt trapped at her place of employment, and the reasons for this became clearer when she explained that she received the health insurance benefits for herself and her children through the store.

She also felt that if she left the store, she would have no friends at all because she didn't have much experience in developing friendships. Her prior friendships had been through her husband and later the ones she made on the job. She didn't feel confident enough to join a club or organization or to seek out other people's company.

Lynn certainly needed to re-evaluate her situation and come up with a plan to take responsibility for her life. The first issue Lynn had to address was to admit that she had been spending way too freely on frivolous items and to stop it immediately – accepting reality. Another related painful realization was that she was simply paying way too much in rent for her budget. On some level, she knew this but had felt overwhelmed by having to admit it since it forced her to take action. Once she made the decision, however, it didn't take her long to find a more suitable place to live.

Feeling trapped in the job situation was going to take a little more time to address. Without alternative skills and with three teenagers to support, it certainly made no sense for her to impulsively quit her job. So, I referred her for some vocational testing and in discussing her interests and the dreams she had when she was younger, I learned that she really liked being around children and had always dreamed that she might become a teacher.

Lynn enrolled part-time in college at night, and of course, what do you think automatically happened? She began to make friends with some other older adult students, something she told me had never come naturally to her. There were times when Lynn felt really frustrated and not as bright as many of the students, and she found she had to take advantage of the labs and tutoring opportunities at the college. However, once again, when she went for assistance, she found herself connecting with other older students like herself and consequently not feeling so alone or so insecure about her abilities.

She still disliked her job as a cashier at the grocery store, but she found it was a little more tolerable because she was in the process of moving forward, in the midst of a plan for taking responsibility for her future. When she explored the requirements for teaching in the school system, she found that there were some teacher's aide jobs that she might be qualified for. She looked into it, found that there were some openings, and applied.

Because she had indicated that she was willing to work in classrooms with children with special needs, she obtained a position fairly quickly. To her surprise, she found that she qualified immediately for the health care benefits. She happily said goodbye to the job she had disliked for so long. Energized by working in a new environment, she was able to continue to go to school at night to pursue her degree. It would be a while before she could obtain her degree and become a teacher, but the goal was in sight.

In a relatively short period of time, Lynn accepted responsibility and took some decisive action for herself and began to give her life new direction. The job that she thought had her trapped only had her trapped when she avoided making some difficult, painful decisions. Once she made them, doors started to open and she began to build a *better* life for herself after divorce. *We always have choices.* Are you on the lookout for opportunities to get what you say your really want out of life?

Let's use Lynn's story again to look at what she *didn't* do:

- She didn't expect her environment to change; she did the changing.

- Lynn didn't blame anyone else for her situation, especially her former spouse.

- She didn't blame the store for her unhappiness – she knew *she* could not be happy there even though some other people could be.

- She didn't complain that the store didn't pay her enough; she realized she needed to make more money elsewhere.

- She didn't complain that her landlord charged too much money.

- She didn't say her husband paid too little in child support.

- She didn't attribute her financial problems to the cash settlement not being large enough.

- She didn't blame others for not seeking out her friendship. She took responsibility for her own life.

Let's not overlook the terrific added bonus in this story of Lynn's life – think of the wonderful life lessons she was teaching her three children as they observed their mother growing and getting *better* while navigating through this process!

What areas of your life are you solely responsible for and are *avoiding* attending to? Have you always promised yourself that you would exercise and get in shape? Are you eating poorly and just hoping you'll get away with it?

Do you tend to take your health for granted simply because there hasn't yet been a health crisis? *Now* is the perfect time to address this issue, right when you need all the physical benefits of exercising and eating right for stress reduction.

You may already be thinking that you can't possibly effectively reduce your stress level now, that its out of your control. But you can, especially if you decide to make stress reduction a priority and that you will take responsibility for yourself. So, use the event of your divorce to get clear on *your intentions.* This means you don't live by accident or coincidence, you live *on purpose*. This is the perfect time to explore this while your intentions are not confused by a partner's intentions.

One way in which to take charge of your life and to live on purpose is to decide that you will incorporate some fun into your life. Are you having any fun? You also need to design a life that has some peace. You may be thinking that these issues are not critical at this point in your life and are also somewhat contradictory to the experience of going through a divorce. But, if you are in charge of your life, you must design it to include fun and peace. You are entitled to these. No one else is going to do it for you, especially if your former spouse was the one who dictated what "fun" was. Taking responsibility for yourself and your life doesn't mean that you work on *surviving* your divorce, it means *thriving* through your divorce!

Another pitfall along the way of learning to take responsibility for yourself and your intentions is to consciously or unconsciously focus on taking too much responsibility for someone else's life. Are you spending time worrying whether your former spouse can "make it alone"? This is not an uncommon phenomenon, especially if your ex had problems with substance abuse or a depressed mood or difficulty holding on to a job.

Of course he or she will "make it", if they *choose* to do so – just like you. This is not your role; you are not the boss of their life. So stop accepting responsibility for your former spouse's life decisions. Accept responsibility for your part in the demise of your marriage and let your ex accept responsibility for theirs.

Along with the above, being personally responsible and "better" post-divorce also includes treating your ex-spouse like an adult. It even means treating them fairly behind their back when they are not around to hear what you have to say. Think about it – isn't it amazing how many people you've heard or overheard talking about their wicked, abominable ex-spouse? (Have you done it yourself?) It sounds as if there must be millions of truly despicable formerly married individuals out there who single-handedly destroyed a marriage if we are to believe the characterizations we hear!

This isn't reality – it's just easier, a way of avoiding introspection and accountability for whatever part you played in the demise of your marriage.

As most of us must honestly admit, very rarely is one individual solely responsible for the breakup of a marriage. But, just for the sake of argument, lets say that you were absolutely faultless in your marriage and one day out of the blue, your spouse simply went insane and ran away with someone, never to be heard from again. So here you are now, abandoned, left without a partner and they are totally to blame.

Guess what? *You are still accountable for yourself and your behavior.* You married that person, and now you have to take responsibility, or accountability, for how you are going to live the rest of your life even if they abandoned you.

Using this admittedly exaggerated example, in which your former spouse would be *totally to blame*, was it unfair? Sure. Was it hurtful? Yes. Would you likely be in shock? Yes, initially. Did you choose that person as a partner? Yes. Despite this, you are still left to make sense of what happened to you and still accountable for your life. No matter what the specific circumstances are, you cannot change the history of your marriage.

Blaming even someone who appears to be totally culpable simply won't help you to get on with responsibly constructing a *better* life. Taking responsibility for yourself means actively confronting issues, dealing with them, wiping the slate clean, and then moving on. Whether you remain single or enter into another marriage, you must accept responsibility for your own happiness. You must examine your thoughts in order to deal with your feelings, because what you tell yourself will determine the choices you then make and the consequences you will ultimately end up with – positive or negative; *bitter or better*.

Chapter 4

Your Finances After Divorce

"The great thing in this world is not so much where you stand, as in what direction you are moving."

Oliver Wendell Holmes, Jr.

Money is a powerful and often painful, anxiety-laden subject. Money and issues related to money are an integral part of our lives, and it is pretty well accepted that money issues in and of themselves are a major contributing cause to many divorces. So what better time than right now to evaluate your financial health, even if money issues were not a significant contributor to the break up of your marriage. After a divorce, most people would be well advised to take the time to assess their current financial situation. Consider the following questions:

- How did you or your partner use money during the marriage?

- Did you spend money carelessly or recklessly because you felt you had someone else to lean on?
- What was your investment style? Were you happy with it? Did it produce the results you wanted?
- During your marriage, did you put off saving money?
- Who paid the bills when you were married?
- Is paying the bills a new responsibility for you?
- Do you feel that financial decisions within your previous marriage were controlled by your former spouse? Is this reality or are you just blaming him or her?

I assure you, if it's not reality and you just feel better blaming your former spouse for any financial difficulties you had in the marriage, you will learn NOTHING by blaming your former spouse.

Although you may have complaints that are factual about how money was managed (or mismanaged) in your marriage, complaining or explaining that "my husband handled all the money", "my wife was a clothes horse", "my husband never paid our taxes on time", or "I just couldn't get my wife to stop charging expensive vacations"(did you accompany her on those vacations?) really doesn't matter any more, does it, since you are no longer married to that individual. It may provide a partial explanation for your current financial status, but once again, I'll ask you "now what are you going to do about it?"

Sometimes, the dysfunctional patterns we had in the marriage regarding money really do not become fully apparent to us until we are divorced. Let me give you the best example I have of this from a very close friend of mine.

Pat and her husband led a pretty comfortable financial life when they were married because both were doctors. They had different specialties, and Pat's husband had been in practice longer and was in a higher-paying specialty area. Throughout their 20-year marriage, Pat had developed what was initially an unconscious pattern of running out and buying herself an expensive piece of jewelry in response to having an argument with her husband. Over time, she engaged in this behavior deliberately.

When they divorced, Pat had one heck of a jewelry collection and a suddenly reduced income as a single wage earner in a much less lucrative specialty area. Along with this came the inescapable realization that she had been engaging in a rather unhealthy habit that she could no longer afford to support every time she got upset in a relationship. It took some honesty on her part to acknowledge that she had punished her husband by indulgently spending money when she felt he had hurt her.

Now, I am a psychologist, not a financial planner. This discussion of your finances is not intended to help you make specific financial decisions but instead to draw your attention to the fact that after going through a divorce, undoubtedly a unique opportunity presents itself to examine your financial life more closely (if you accept the challenge). Avoiding unresolved financial issues could be consuming as much or even more emotional energy than if you were to just deal with those issues. It just *seems* easier to put off dealing with your financial health, but its not.

Do you worry about money? Are you plagued by nagging thoughts about unpaid bills, mounting credit card debt, or other financial issues you haven't yet resolved? Do financial worries represent the bulk of your final thoughts as you fall asleep at night or are they the first things that pop into your head when you wake up? That's what can happen with unresolved issues, and if this is true for you, then you need to put a plan into action.

Financial goals are no different than other goals you might set. You won't reach them without a deliberate plan – your choices *now* will produce the consequences later – good or bad. Right now is the perfect time to start identifying what you need your money to do for you. I know, some of you are saying "but I don't have any money to do anything with!" In this case, you need to back up a step and start with a plan that will help you to have more money to begin with.

Let me ask you some questions to get you thinking about the financial issues I'm referring to:

- Do you have a child's college education to save for? Have you started?

- Have you thought about when you want to retire? How are you going to do it?

- Do you have credit card debt you'd like to pay off? If so, do you know when you want it paid off?

- Do you want to own your own home or a different home than the one you have now?

- Do you need to develop a system for paying your bills on time so that those creditors will stop calling you?

- Do you need life insurance and haven't gotten around to it?

- If you have life insurance, do you know who the beneficiary is? Could it still be listed as your former spouse? (a common oversight)

- If you have children, should you have a will drawn up or set up a trust?

- Do you need to get a copy of your credit report and examine it for errors or clean it up?

- Are you fully funding your retirement accounts? If not, why?

- Do you have disability insurance? Do you need it?

- Do you even know how much money you have available in cash right now? When did you last balance your checkbook?

- Do you bounce checks?

- Does someone owe you money but you neglect to ask for it?

If your finances are the area of your life where you have tended to be irresponsible or passive in the past or have allowed a partner to take control, now is the time to take a serious look at these issues. Finances are about responsibility, and marriages typically end because one or both of the partners was irresponsible in some fashion in one or more areas of their life. Being fiscally immature or irresponsible is an area of neglect that will haunt you forever.

Financial situations *do not* fix themselves – they require corrective action. Not wishing, hoping, dreaming, or talking about them but *acting* upon them. If your financial life is out of control, I guarantee that *you* will feel anxious and out of control. If you have no answers right now to many of the questions posed above, by all means, get a pen and a piece of paper and start writing down all the financial concerns you have, prioritize them, and *get someone to help you!*

Now you are going to ask **who** should help you. Actually, the answer is quite simple. Look around you at the people you know who have their financial lives in order, people you admire and respect. It might be a parent, an uncle, a neighbor, a co-worker, a friend, but hopefully you know someone who seems to have successfully handled at least some of these issues. Be careful, though, because looks can be deceiving.

Don't just ask the person who is driving the nicest car or seems to have the most money to spend. Plenty of people look like they are doing just fine but have no savings, no plans for the future, plenty of credit-card debt, and are about a week away from filing for bankruptcy. Ask someone you know and trust. There are also nonprofit debt-management organizations that can help you. And if you aren't comfortable sharing your particular personal situation, just ask people you trust for a recommendation for an accountant or a financial planner. I'm always happy to refer people to my accountant, and you'll probably find that others are pleased to do so as well.

Make sure that you feel comfortable with this person, that you feel their fees are affordable for you, and that they have experience with situations such as yours.

One of the most immediately rewarding actions I took soon after my divorce was finalized began when I requested a copy of my credit report. I found *five* significant errors that I was able to have corrected and found *eleven* old, open, forgotten, unused credit accounts just sitting there, all of which I promptly had cancelled at my request. This was not a cumbersome task – much of it was handled by some brief telephone calls, and the rest involved filling out a simple form to document the errors. The result? Accurate information about my credit history and perhaps more importantly at the time, an instantaneous sense of greater control over my new life.

Lets go back to that concern about simply not having enough money. Unfortunately, the vast majority of people go through a divorce and come out on the other side feeling much poorer. In fact, the latest statistics from the National Center for Health Statistics report that 45% of women in the United States experience a significant decrease in their standard of living following divorce.

There's no doubt about it – divorces cost lots of money, both in legal fees and expenses and in reduced income. You may have some debt now that you didn't anticipate. We have all heard of a story of a divorce that cost way more money than ours did, but whatever the particular financial cost of your divorce was, that's the one you've got to deal with. It probably doesn't really make you feel much better to know that someone else spent even more money to end a marriage.

So what can you do about not having enough money? Again, I'm not a financial planner, but I can guarantee you what the first step should be. **Honestly evaluate your situation.** Most of us had to fill out that tedious financial affidavit during the divorce process. Do it again for yourself now that you aren't married. Go through the same process. I know, you're saying, "I just don't have enough money" or "I just don't make enough money," or "I'm not receiving enough child support", it has nothing to do with a financial affidavit." It has *everything* to do with it – with understanding exactly what your situation really is – how much money is coming in and where you are spending every dollar.

I can remember filling out that lengthy form. What I remember most is being prompted to think about things that probably wouldn't have occurred to me on my own, such as the category about expenses for your pets and how much you spend on getting your hair cut or on your children's vitamins. The task seemed a bit daunting at the time, but it was definitely illuminating.

This is about facing facts. You absolutely cannot solve your problem of not having enough money if you delude yourself about this and aren't honest about where your starting point is. Could it be that perhaps you really do have enough money, but you're just spending it in the wrong places?

If this is the case, its unlikely that you are going to want to admit this to yourself, but I presume if you are continuing to read this book, you are interested in making a better life for yourself by dealing with the truth about some important matters. So where does your money go? If you force yourself to write it all down, you will have an accurate answer to this question and be in a much better position to make the necessary adjustments.

Like all other areas of our lives, getting a genuine handle on exactly what we are currently doing is the reality that can get our attention and provoke us to make the necessary changes. For example, how many times have you heard of the weight loss strategy of keeping a log or diary of every single thing you eat before or during an attempt to begin a new diet? You may have done this yourself at some point in your life.

There is sound reasoning behind that strategy – most of us would *not* accurately know what we ingest on a daily basis – we human beings tend to minimize or underestimate. The process of paying attention to it, writing it down, and acknowledging what we see on paper illuminates the problem areas and facilitates developing a plan to correct the problem.

The same principle applies to your finances. You need to know exactly how much money is coming in and exactly how much money is going out and where it is going before you can make any necessary adjustments. If this is a problematic area of your life, I urge you to do your own financial affidavit before you ask someone else to help you with a plan to get your finances in order.

What if you have assessed your current situation honestly and have concluded that you simply do not have enough income to meet your financial obligations and to support a reasonable lifestyle? Well, the obvious solution is to first trim some areas of expense. We are all capable of trimming in some areas. As a matter of fact, at the time that I am writing this, I am still driving the only used car I ever bought – the car I bought *after* my divorce, which is what made the most financial sense at that time in my life. But what if a more significant change is required now that you are divorced?

Do you need to re-evaluate how you earn your income and your earning potential? From a financial standpoint, are you in the right job? Could you be doing the right job but in the wrong company? Could it be possible that you need some type of a career change or more marketable skills? Do you need to obtain further education? This is the perfect time to take a serious look at these issues and to develop a plan to deal with them.

Let me tell you how my friend Sheila successfully addressed this issue. Sheila had been working as an administrative assistant at a junior high school when she went through her divorce. Although she liked her work environment in the school setting, after about a year as a single parent of a thirteen year old and an eleven year old, she realized that her income was inadequate for her active lifestyle with her children, for their future educational needs as well as her retirement, and there was really no opportunity for advancement at the school. So, she came up with a plan to develop more skills and to increase her earning potential while continuing with the financial security of her job as an administrative assistant.

Sheila completed a two-year paralegal program at night while working full-time during the day. Immediately upon graduation, she was hired by the local family court system in her county and was able to increase her income and was also thrilled to be able to work in an area of law that served abused children. She didn't complain about her financial situation, make excuses, and wish for a new job opportunity to appear. Sheila assessed her situation, developed a purposeful plan, and took action.

Earlier I told you that the first step was an honest assessment of your situation. Well, that's only the first step. It's an absolutely necessary step in acknowledging where you are coming from, but it doesn't set any activities in motion. To move into a position of *better* requires *action*. You must *do* things *differently*. Sheila began to build a *better* life because she didn't just think about her situation or talk about it; she took responsibility for her life and *did it*.

What areas of your financial life are in need of some action on your part right now? Make a list and prioritize them by urgency. Then make a plan to do the items on the list, one at a time. It could be as simple, but necessary, as finding out how much money you have right now in your checking account. Just do it. Don't concern yourself even for a minute with being embarrassed – it's a waste of energy. I can assure you that you won't be the first person to walk into your bank and ask them how much money you *really* have in your account.

I promise you that when you take action in even simple financial areas of your life, you will find that a wonderful kind of rewarding momentum will develop as you *do* things differently, and you will want to keep taking decisive action in order to maintain that feeling.

One of my patients was doing quite well working on various aspects of his life a few years after his divorce, but his financial life was certainly not in good shape. He had never felt successful in financial areas. He had a nagging concern that he simply could not escape – he finally revealed to me that he had not filed an income tax return in several years.

He had no idea how much money he might owe, and he was literally losing sleep over the uncertainty. He had made some tremendous changes in his life, but avoiding this issue threatened to sabotage his overall success. It was no longer acceptable to use the excuse that his former wife had handled these matters or that he just didn't have enough financial knowledge.

Although he really wanted to have a comprehensive plan for his future, he simply had not been honest with himself about this issue and resisted addressing it directly. Over time he recognized that this unresolved problem in his life would either remain a constant source of anxiety or would eventually get resolved by the IRS in a manner which would be outside of his control (and which would probably cause even more anxiety!) It became increasingly clear that he would have to acknowledge the situation and take personal responsibility for taking action.

Repeatedly, I urged him to meet with an accountant to get real and face the facts about how bad his situation really was. Finally, he confronted his own anxiety, took my advice and found an accountant who had been an IRS agent – just the right guy to help him evaluate his situation. They quickly came up with a plan to address the delinquent tax returns.

They filed the tax returns one at a time, and it proved to be fairly painless. In fact, during the years when he wasn't managing his finances, he also wasn't making very much money and so he didn't even owe any money! What was so impressive, though, was that once those tax returns were dealt with – once he had accepted the facts and taken action, the immediate reduction of anxiety freed him to address other financial concerns and soon he had opened a savings account and an IRA and re-established his credit.

He took this action a few years ago, and the financial progress he has made is tremendous. No more anxiety about the IRS – in fact, he still uses the same accountant and continues to get a kick out of filing his income tax return as early as possible. Only *you* can really address your own financial situation – do something innovative – use your divorce as the impetus to take charge of your financial life.

Chapter 5

Relationship Lessons From a Marriage That Didn't Work

"The heart has its reasons which reason does not know."

Blaise Pascal

You are reading this book because your marriage is over or it is ending. Regardless of the specific reason(s) why your marriage ended, I believe you do need to understand why you chose that partner. I'm not talking about the specifics of what your former spouse did, but rather about gaining some insight into how your life experiences contributed to your previous choices so that you can utilize that information today to make a conscious, healthy choice in a new romantic partner.

There are no accidents in whom you have found attractive in the past and who has found you to be attractive. You didn't *coincidentally* get married. In fact, you probably have some conception in your mind of your "type" of ideal mate. You didn't get married because of some sort of bad luck, and I don't believe that there are any "arranged" marriages in this country anymore. I continue to be amazed at the discrepancy in what people *tell me* they are or were looking for in a partner and then what they seem surprised to have ended up with. What you want in a partner really tends to be the qualities you want in yourself.

If you ever intend to be involved in an intimate, committed relationship again, and I certainly hope you do, this is not a time for *what you don't know won't hurt you* – what you don't know about the factors that shape your choices absolutely can and will hurt you! If you don't pay attention to this issue and choose to delude yourself, you are at risk for making similar choices because sadly, as you probably already know, second marriages end in divorce again at an alarmingly high rate.

If your previous marriage or long-term relationships were characterized by the same recurring problems, you must take a look at what you do to allow, reinforce, or encourage unhealthy behavior. It is highly likely that if you look honestly at your past relationships, you will identify some disconcerting patterns. Without approaching this area of your life with conscious intentions, you could begin dating and unconsciously pick a new partner who will allow you to feel comfortable, as if you are in your former marriage – remember that old comfort zone I told you about?

First, you've got to take a look at what stage you are in right now as you contemplate dating and developing a romantic relationship. What are your thoughts about the opposite sex? Are you still angry? Are you in any way longing for your former husband or wife? If so, please don't start dating yet! It's not fair to you or to that potential dating partner. You've got some work to do. You've got to like yourself again – or like yourself for the first time if you're not sure you ever did in the first place. You've got to get comfortable with yourself first.

This point should go without saying, but in my opinion, its not advantageous to start dating while you are still married. It may seem to some of you like you're getting a jump on things, but you've still got enough to work on without prematurely entering the dating world. It's a complication that you really don't need. I distinctly remember what my attorney told me so profoundly during the process of my divorce, "you're married until you're not married". It's true – you are either married or you aren't; it's either over or it isn't.

Do you feel like you *must* date? If so, why? Is it because of pressure from other people? Do you feel like you need to date, or are family members and friends urging you to do so? There can be a lot of societal pressure, and you may feel compelled to start dating as people offer to "fix you up". Romance will not fix you.

Does it feel as if the single cure for loneliness is to begin dating? Does it feel like a *need* to you, or are you just feeling ready to get out there and socialize? If you're ready to socialize, that's wonderful, as long as that doesn't mean drowning your sorrows in beer on a stool at the local bar. If the prospect of dating makes you feel particularly anxious, simply begin by socializing in a group – you know, the way you probably first approached dating when you were in high school and felt uncertain. Its amazing how this dating process after having been married sure can make you feel like an awkward high school student again!

Believe it or not, there is definitely something to be

said about the benefit of the *process* of the divorce, even though we often cannot perceive the benefit at the time. There exists some kind of subtle pressure to hurry through it, as if we can skip over some of the painful parts. It's natural to want to omit some of the stages. The various emotional stages in the process are not right or wrong in and of themselves. The risk in navigating through the process is that without consciously choosing to be *better*, you could wallow too long in any one emotional stage and stop moving forward.

The entire process of my divorce from the initial filing of the papers until the final decree took about sixteen months. At the time, I felt like my divorce was definitely in slow motion and was going to be the longest one on record! I distinctly remember feeling like my soon-to-be ex-husband was somehow responsible for slowing down the natural process of my life. I wanted it to just be over. In my particular case, the date of the final divorce hearing was even reset twice, delaying it by another month – I began to feel like it would never occur.

However, in retrospect, I am thankful for those sixteen months, and I wouldn't change it by even a day. Somehow, it is exactly what needed to happen. I didn't know it when I was going through it, but I desperately needed that time for adjustment. During that time I had packed, and moved, and gradually unpacked. It gave me time to go through boxes of photographs and to sort through those that I would later give to my ex-husband.

Those sixteen months were my initiation into learning to spend every other weekend alone in my townhouse without my children. It gave me time to meet my new neighbors and make some new friends. I got to decide how I wanted to spend my 38th birthday. I initiated becoming more active in my church. I got reacquainted with the fun of going out to dinner with a girlfriend. I played music that only I wanted to listen to.

It was during that period of time that I first really read the Bible. It was during those sixteen months that I genuinely contemplated what my role in the marriage had been and what part I had played in its demise. I had time to think about my own relationship patterns and to dare to contemplate what I really needed and wanted from a future relationship. And it was during that period of time that I realized I could make a conscious decision to transform myself, that it was totally up to me to decide to become *better* from this experience and to not be angry or bitter. I had to simply *be* in that phase, and I sincerely believe that it is a critical process that is much more easily accomplished while not encumbered with dating or trying to start another relationship.

Perhaps you are the kind of person that has *always* been in a relationship. You *always* had a boyfriend or girlfriend. You can't go any length of time without being in a romantic relationship. In fact, if you look back on them, you might characterize most of your relationships as "rebound" relationships. When my daughter was a senior in high school, I distinctly remember one of her girlfriends. This young woman was attractive, energetic, intelligent, and generally fun to be around. She was ambitious and competent, and it appeared that she had a great future ahead of her.

I also remember my daughter commenting on this young woman's boyfriends, and they all seemed to be nice guys. However, my daughter was talking to me one day about her girfriend's latest breakup and commented, "you know, Mom, she *has* to have a boyfriend." We discussed how odd it seemed at first that such a confident, busy girl just had to have a boyfriend all the time.

But the more we discussed it and the more I thought about it, it began to make sense. We rarely spent any time with my daughter's friend – she often just breezed through our house. In fact, she was always on her way to somewhere else. My daughter began to realize that the essence of their friendship occurred only in brief phone conversations – cell phone conversations, as she was never at home. She was usually too busy to do what my daughter wanted and seemed to run from activity to activity. Not a day went by that this girl didn't have a boyfriend. I suspect that she felt chronically empty and constantly needed somebody or something in order to temporarily address the issues that she had not yet confronted in herself.

When the time arises, I frequently talk to my divorced patients who are entertaining the idea of dating again for the first time or exploring new romantic relationships about being alert to "red flags" and have found it to be a very useful metaphor. I advise the people I work with to respond honestly and quickly to the presence of "red flags" or warning signs, rather than waiting for an accumulation of evidence and investing in a relationship where they will ultimately be hurt. There are "red flags" that I believe are almost universal, and then there are those "red flags" that are unique to the individual because of their personal experiences.

The universal red flags are things such as a partner with a chemical addiction, the person who isn't truly available (i.e., because they are married to someone else!), a potential partner who has frequent anger or "rages", the person who is still very emotionally connected to an ex-mate either in anger or longing to be with them and can't let go of the past, or the person who is financially irresponsible.

The universal red flag of becoming involved with

someone with a chemical addiction is a straightforward problem and one that I'm admittedly painfully blunt about. The person you choose to be involved with who has an addiction to drugs or alcohol is already committed to a relationship with those substances prior to any relationship with you. They are "in love" with the drugs and/or alcohol, so essentially you are signing up to be involved in a love triangle. This may be a personal red flag for you if your former spouse had an addiction that was a major contributing factor to the ending of your marriage. It is well known that relationships are constantly destroyed by addictions.

In my clinical practice, I have repeatedly witnessed the hurt and destruction caused by a partner's abuse or addiction to a substance. I must admit, though, I cannot recall a relationship where the partner without the addiction wasn't aware of the abuse or addiction of their partner right at the beginning of the relationship and chose to ignore or minimize it, made excuses for it, or thought they would "change" their partner's behavior.

Let me tell you about Janine's situation. Janine would be considered an intelligent and extremely competent woman by anyone's standards. She is an R.N. and went on to earn a masters degree in nursing. She comes from a good, loving family and is attractive, physically fit, and has many interests and friends. Janine was married to John for eight years and although she truly wanted children, she told me that she always had an uncomfortable feeling that perhaps her marriage would not last because of her husband's drinking problem and so she put off having children. A physically active woman, Janine had met John at a gym and had been attracted to him initially in part because he was physically fit.

She also knew before she married him that he liked to

"party" and drank quite a bit. During their marriage, John drank more and more, became increasingly depressed and irritable, and spent much less time with her. At times, she literally found herself begging him to participate in healthy activities with her such as golf and horseback riding. When they were together in public, he tended to embarrass her with his behavior as he would quickly become drunk and then openly and loudly critical of her.

His drinking continued, and she immersed herself in obtaining another college degree. Her instincts were correct, and eventually her husband's drinking became clearly more important than the marriage. He refused to get any help, and they divorced. She handled the break-up of that marriage quite well, and it was when she was contemplating getting married again a few years later that she came to see me.

When Janine sought therapy, she had been seriously involved with Roger for nine months, and they were talking about getting married. However, there were red flags about the relationship that she had not admitted to anyone. Roger was a drinker also, but Janine was now thirty-nine years old and emphasized that she really did want to get married and have a child.

She admitted that her parents had recently visited and had met Roger and had voiced some concerns to her. Roger tended to avoid resolving issues and would become increasingly irritable when he drank, frequently storming out of the house when confronted. He accused her of trying to control his behavior, and occasionally she found hidden bottles of liquor in their apartment. Roger was less responsible at home than when they had first moved in together and she found herself silently feeling resentful. Privately, Janine admitted to me that sometimes she felt like she had to manage everything as if she were Roger's mother.

It was obvious that Janine was in a lot of denial about the painful similarities between her previous marriage and her current relationship. She even went so far as to talk about the changes she could make that might "make him change". Of course, their relationship had already reached the stage where when confronted about his drinking, Roger would blame Janine in some way such as "if you weren't so ____, I wouldn't drink so much". No one *makes* anyone drink or use drugs – such comments from a partner are a pitiful excuse and a definite red flag.

But the real key that enabled Janine to see how doomed her relationship with Roger was and how it was so clearly a re-enactment from the past came when she honestly stated out loud in therapy "I'm so lonely". When your partner is addicted to any substance, they cannot be emotionally available and committed to you, and therefore, you will end up feeling lonely even while in the midst of a relationship.

Janine did finally give him an ultimatum, and she subsequently took the initiative to go to an Al-Anon meeting. Roger chose to continue drinking, however, and Janine had to make the courageous and painful decision to follow through with her ultimatum and end the relationship. Had Janine originally been on the lookout for those red flags, she might have been able to avoid becoming so invested in a hurtful relationship by ending the relationship early on when she recognized his drinking behavior or at least when he initially refused to stop abusing alcohol.

Let's talk a bit about that potential partner who is unavailable. Pursuing a partner who is not really available to you should make a big red flag start waving. For those of you who have made the mistake in the past of choosing someone who cannot commit because they were involved in another relationship, this is a personal red flag for you as well as a universal one and you know *exactly* what I'm talking about. And if you are really honest with yourself, you will recall that probably *no one* but you thought that the relationship with that unavailable person was a good idea or had any promise.

I've always been fascinated when a patient has asked me what I think about pursuing a relationship with a married man or woman and tries to get me to buy into their rationalization of why they aren't going to get hurt (frankly, they probably regret asking me since I don't tell them what they want to hear). Here's my simple advice: if you're contemplating this kind of relationship, don't do it; if you are in a relationship with someone that's married, get some self-respect, do the right thing, and end it. Period.

I know this sounds harsh, and I know that those of you to whom this part of the book applies are most likely starting to form objections beginning with "but, ...". So let me explain why the advice is *so* incredibly simple. When you choose to be in a relationship with someone who is unavailable (which is barely a relationship because the other person is involved in a separate committed relationship), you are announcing what you think you deserve in a relationship – second-best, leftovers, taking whatever you can get, something is better than nothing – you can call it by any term you like but this is exactly what it is.

Everyone deserves better than this. No one should agree to be in an intimate relationship where they know they are not a priority in the other person's life. The painful question you must ask yourself is "why am I willing to settle?" When you agree to be involved in such a relationship, you are instructing the other person about how you are willing to be treated - poorly.

Just so you are perfectly clear about this issue, I am not only referring to dating someone who is married but about all the other forms of "unavailability" such as: the person who is in a relationship but insists that they really aren't "in love" with that person, someone who admits they have only a sexual relationship with another person but its really just sex and not a "relationship", and even the person who says they are going to file for divorce or just filed for divorce. None of these situations involve people who are truly free to be in a relationship with you – they are still involved and are likely to remain involved.

If being involved with someone who is unavailable to commit to you is a pattern which you identify from your past or you now find yourself drawn into such a relationship, you must do some self-examination about why this would be acceptable to you. It is a potentially agonizing situation and damaging to your self-esteem. In fact, it really demonstrates that you likely have so little self-esteem that this is all you feel you are entitled to in a relationship. When these relationships fail, and inevitably the overwhelming majority of them do, you cannot blame your partner for having betrayed you.

Lets just suppose for a moment that you're a woman dating a married man who eventually does in fact leave his wife in order to be with you – would you really trust that he's committed to you? How would you know? He wasn't committed to his last partner, and she likely thought he was. Do you really want to be in a relationship with someone who is untrustworthy and/or lacking in integrity? Don't settle or sell out now while you are on the verge of establishing a *better* life.

So how do you know if that incredible lack of patience or rapidly changing, volatile mood from the guy you are dating is really a red flag? I hear patients frequently and casually use the nonclinical term "rageaholic" to refer to individuals with chronic anger problems. How do you know if the person you are becoming involved with has a serious problem with anger?

In my opinion, if you are even silently *questioning* whether someone has a serious problem, you've already encountered some of the warning signs but probably don't want to admit it yet to yourself. Let me give you some concrete red flags that indicate the person you are involved with or are contemplating becoming involved with has a major anger problem:

§ They can't wait in line, wait for service, can't tolerate traffic, or stand to be put on hold

§ They easily resort to name-calling when thwarted (towards you or others)

§ They have no compunction about becoming loud and angry in public

§ They act out by hanging up the phone, storming out of rooms, the house, or public places, or slam doors

§ They throw objects, hit things, or shove or strike people

There are many reasons why someone you are involved with may have a serious anger management problem or be a "rageaholic" – they likely were abused as a child in some fashion, they may have had alcoholic parents, or any number of other reasons. This may sound harsh, but you know what? Why they are this way really doesn't matter right now. You are not their therapist. In my clinical experience, the partner of the "rageaholic" is always much more interested in understanding the origins of their partner's anger and trying to help them deal with their feelings than the person who is engaging in all the angry, unacceptable behavior.

Don't ask yourself why they act this way. Ask yourself "why would I choose to put up with such behavior". And then my question to you, as usual, will be "what are you going to do about it?" It's a gigantic red flag, and if you notice that you seem to *attract* angry partners, you can't afford to spend an extra day of your life being the target of such behavior. The better investment is for you to spend some time and effort on figuring out why you are unconsciously drawn to angry people and why you would tolerate such interactions so that you can *choose* not to do so anymore.

You will remember that in Chapter 4, we addressed financial issues after divorce. Financial irresponsibility is one of those universal red flags as well as a frequent personal red flag for many people. You may have done a good job of honestly addressing your own financial situation, but if you are a rescuer or you are willing to rationalize someone else's mistakes, the area of financial irresponsibility can be a red flag that you may lapse into ignoring. I can't tell you how many men and women I have heard make excuses that their boyfriend, girlfriend, husband, or wife is "just not very good with money" as they explain how he or she doesn't answer their phone to avoid the bill collectors.

When you are getting to know someone and early in the relationship he or she needs to borrow a significant sum of money from you – *red flag!* When your partner spends money on unnecessary luxuries but can't pay his rent – *red flag!* If your partner jokes about bouncing checks – *red flag!* If the person you are dating explains that he doesn't pay his child support in full or on time because he really doesn't think his former spouse needs it – *red flag!*

People who are financially irresponsible tend to have other areas in their life in which they are irresponsible as well. It's a major form of neglect, and if you are truly working on making your life *better* after the ordeal of divorce, this is *not* an area where you want to compromise.

Don't ignore the red flag of financial irresponsibility. To ignore it means that you are signing up to be that person's financial advisor, loan officer, and/or surrogate parent – a sure way to get yourself involved in an unhealthy relationship with someone who hasn't decided to be a grown-up yet.

What about when the person you are dating talks a lot about their former spouse – either positively or with tremendous anger? Neither situation is a good one. This could be the red flag of a partner who is too emotionally connected to their ex. It's a rather obvious cause for concern when you notice that your new dating partner expresses a considerable amount of anger towards people or events from the past.

There are really two kinds of red flags here – the person you are dating who has tremendous anger or hatred towards their former spouse may eventually project those feelings onto you or your new partner may seem to be so traumatized by their ex that they are unable to be in a new relationship and you spend all of your energy trying to make things "right" for them, trying to heal them, and in effect, trying to *rescue* them. Once again, you are not their therapist.

On the other hand, some individuals can be emotionally connected to their former marriage in a wistful, longing-for-the-past kind of way. Some people don't seem to know how to let go, the attachment lingers, and there may never be a complete break. Some people you meet may lack proper boundaries with their former spouse and may demonstrate this by taking unnecessary responsibility for their ex or constantly remaining in contact. Much to your confusion, they may even repeatedly remind you about all the wonderful qualities of their former spouse.

They may even try to shield their ex-spouse from the knowledge that they are dating or involved in a relationship, and consequently, your existence may be hidden from your partner's ex because he or she feels they can't let them know. Obviously, this is a red flag and doesn't provide the foundation for a healthy relationship. If the person you are seeing is maintaining an unnecessary level of attachment to their ex, they are likely to be unable to experience a full, new relationship with you. If you are the one who is clinging to the opportunities to see your former mate, reminiscing about the past, and stopping over to offer to make repairs on your old house, be aware that you are stifling your personal growth and delaying your personal happiness.

A very easy pitfall is to date someone who is totally different from your ex simply because they are just that – totally different. Whatever characteristics your former spouse had, the opposite ones suddenly look quite appealing. It may seem like a good strategy at first, but does it automatically mean that this individual possesses what you need and want in a partner? Of course not. So be alert that while you are immediately relieved that they appear to be the opposite of your former spouse, don't assume that it means they have the qualities required for a healthy relationship.

Let me give you an example of this from my practice. Barbara, as I will call her, had previously been married to a very quiet, subdued man. Barbara has a lot of energy and intensity that you naturally pick up on when you first meet her. She informed me that her first marriage was somewhat unremarkable, boring, and lacking in excitement but didn't have any major problems until she suddenly found out that her husband was seeing another woman. She confronted him and ended the marriage.

After her marriage ended, she had a couple of years to process what had gone wrong in the marriage, and she had concluded that she simply hadn't been married to the right person. She decided that she really needed a man who was more energetic, more active, and with a wider range of interests – someone more like herself. Barbara had numerous interests, a wide range of friends, and was quite athletic.

So, when Barbara met Steve, she immediately felt he was the one for her because he was *totally* different from her ex-husband. He raced boats, he loved to go to parties, he had a motorcycle, and he had similar interests in outdoor activities that she liked. She was enthralled with the excitement of dating Steve, and in fact, they got married after dating for only a few months.

However, when Barbara came to see me, she certainly wasn't focusing on how exciting Steve was compared to her ex-husband. She came to see me because she felt panic-stricken about her marital situation. Steve had been married before as well, but she had never stopped to ask him much about his previous marriage and how the marriage had ended. Steve refused to treat her as an equal partner and to communicate with her about finances.

As Steve continued to spend money indiscriminately in their marriage and the arguments ensued, she asked him about his previous marriage and found out that the house he had owned with his previous wife had gone into foreclosure due to his inability to keep up with making the payments. Suddenly, it made sense to her why Steve had insisted that she obtain the new car loan on their last car based solely on her credit history. She felt desperate for more attention from Steve, but he continued to spend most of his time with his friends in those very activities that Barbara had thought were so intriguing and exciting. Finally, she found that he had a separate, hidden credit card with a large balance which he had not revealed to her.

Barbara had jumped wholeheartedly into a new relationship almost entirely based on Steve appearing to be the opposite of her ex-husband without regard for his other qualities that she got in the bargain. She had been so happy to find a man with qualities that she believed were important to her that she overlooked some very important red flags.

On the other hand, some of you may be avoiding a new relationship because you believe that your marriage, despite its failure, was supposed to be your "one true love". You may believe that there is only one perfect person out there for you. For some reason, many people believe that they get one shot at this, and if it fails, they've used their one chance. Certainly I have found this to be the case for those individuals whose spouse suddenly left them for someone else while they still felt "in love" and had not yet fully processed the real difficulties that existed in the marriage. This is a common phenomenon among some widowed persons who had a really great marriage and now reject future relationships because they had their one longstanding, memorable relationship.

If you believe that there can only be one person for you and you were married to that person, and the marriage failed, where does that leave you? You have automatically cut yourself off to any opportunities for future relationships because of a belief that is probably not rooted in reality.

Of course we are capable of being in a loving relationship with a different person at a different point in our lives. If you are defending against new relationships by clinging to this conviction that there is only one perfect partner for you, you need to examine how you came to have that belief and determine whether it is serving you very well right now. Perhaps it is time to challenge that belief.

Actually, I have found (and I think with time you will, too) that as time goes on and we get some distance and objectivity from the initial emotional pain, if we are truly honest about the details of our failed marriage, most people tend to find that the marriage wasn't nearly as good as we wanted to believe it was when we were originally in shock and began to mourn its loss. The relationship may not have been all that you wanted to believe it was, but you engaged in some level of denial for some time in order to continue it.

Learn from your previous experiences. What you should ideally be looking for at this point in a potential dating partner is an individual who is committed to *growth* – just like I know you are because you are reading this book. Someone who places high value on growing as a human being and who has awareness of their own emotional baggage is willing to ask for and to receive help – as you are demonstrating by reading this book. By this, I mean that you are sensitive to recognizing someone who values self-improvement.

No one comes into a relationship without some degree of emotional baggage, especially not if they have already been married and divorced. Everyone naturally carries his or her own personal history into a relationship. Finding a partner with a total absence of emotional baggage isn't the goal; rather it is finding a partner who has *awareness* of their emotional baggage, acknowledges its potential impact on future relationships, and is readily willing to work on these issues.

Chapter 6

But What About The Children?

"A problem is a chance for you to do your best."

Duke Ellington

In both my personal and clinical experience, worries about the potential impact of divorce on children weigh perhaps the most heavily on adults' minds. This chapter is for those of you who had children with your former spouse and may be wrestling with all the implications that come with being the custodial or non-custodial parent. There are many good resources available that specifically and thoroughly address parenting, co-parenting, and custody and visitation issues. Custody and visitation issues alone are an entire book!

My goal here is not to examine those issues in depth but to point out what I believe are the critical areas and urge you to examine your thoughts and beliefs on these issues. Because concerns about our children is such a challenging part of the aftermath of a divorce, I do want to emphasize that you must make this an aspect of your divorce that fits in with being *better*.

First, you must understand that children are extremely perceptive – make no mistake about this. Depending upon their age, they may not communicate very clearly in a verbal fashion about what they know, but you can be certain that they have known that something was wrong before the divorce itself transpired. In my clinical experience, I have been amazed at what patients have told me had been going on in their house prior to even any filing for divorce and their assertion that their kids really weren't aware. This is ridiculous and naive.

I have worked as a court psychologist for family court, and I have evaluated many children in custody proceedings and continue to do so. Believe me, they know a lot more about your marriage and divorce than you think they know.

A good marital or couples therapist will tell you up front that the goal of couples counseling is not necessarily to keep the couple together. That's right – the goal is to clarify whether the relationship has a strong enough foundation to save it and whether both individuals are committed to strengthening it, and if not, to facilitate the healthiest possible termination of the marriage. Unfortunately, when one or both of the partners believes that remaining married at any cost is in and of itself superior for their children's well being, they are refusing to recognize the effects that their troubled relationship has been having on the children all along.

It's not uncommon for adults to put off getting a divorce and to pick an arbitrary time at which they feel their children can "handle" the divorce, such as when the child goes off to college. Maybe this was how you handled the situation. In my opinion, this is dishonest and sends a confusing message to the child. I must admit that I have yet to meet an adolescent or an adult who later confirmed "gee, I'm so glad Mom and Dad stayed in that lousy, unsatisfying marriage for me and waited to end it until I went off to college!"

If you feel tormented by thoughts of guilt about what your divorce has done to your children, I want you to stop for a moment and think about what your children are no longer exposed to now that you are divorced. The painful truth is that many children live under circumstances where they are relieved to hear that their parents are getting a divorce. Not all children are devastated by the announcement. The following examples may seem extreme to some readers, but unfortunately, they are not all that uncommon. Were your children exposed to:

- Chronic disagreements, arguing, name-calling, shouting and verbal abuse?

- Overhearing discussions about Mommy or Daddy's indiscrete behavior?

- Excessive alcohol or drug use by one of their parents?

- Chronic absence and uninvolvement of one parent allegedly because they "worked late" or were out of town frequently?

- Erratic or confusing behavior because of a parent's emotional problems?

- Pervasive tension and lack of communication in the household?
- Physical abuse of one of their parents?
- Police being called to the house?
- Absence of physical affection between adults?

Once again, let me remind you that your divorce was not an accident. It didn't suddenly occur one day out of the blue with no prior warning, even though you might feel like it occurred that way or may have a strong need to view it that way. Please understand that just as you had prior warning signs about the impending end of your marriage, regardless of the reasons, your children were privy to some of those warning signs consciously or unconsciously as well.

Why am I asking you to think back to these painful circumstances that your children might have been exposed to while I'm trying to move you forward? Because, if you are wasting energy feeling guilty, I want you to pay attention to the benefit your children are receiving from the absence of these experiences as a result of your divorce. It may be hard for you to accept, but children can be healthy and happy in a peaceful, safe home with one healthy parent where they are not exposed to abuse or dysfunctional behavior between their parents.

If you are fortunate to have not had the experiences listed above and you are still feeling guilty, then you must first work on accepting the reality that you are divorced in order to let go of the wasted emotion of guilt. Ask yourself what good your guilt will do for you or your children.

What role is your guilt playing? Will feeling guilty that your children have parents who are divorced make you a better parent?

I don't think so; in fact, I know it won't. Will feeling guilty make your children happier, healthier, better adjusted? Absolutely not. Does feeling guilty help you to become a more emotionally healthy, effective person? You know the answer.

If you are choosing to continue feeling guilty about the impact of your divorce on your children, there has to be some payoff, and the only one I can think of is that you need to punish yourself emotionally. You may not like the way I'm labeling it, but its true. Your guilt serves no other purpose, and in fact it prevents you from acknowledging where you are today and undermines your ability to be an effective parent. You're reading a book entitled *Bitter or Better* – choose guilt and you're eventually choosing *bitter*!

So when it comes to your children and working on being a *better* divorced parent, what aspects of your life do you need to be paying attention to? Briefly answer these questions (honestly!):

- Do you talk negatively about the other parent in front of your children?

- Do you encourage your child's relationship with the other parent?

- Do you sometimes rely on your child as your confidante in place of your partner?

- If you are the non-custodial parent, do you

maintain rather consistent contact with your children?

- Do you exhibit respect for the other parent even when you don't feel like it?

- Do you use your children as a conduit for messages to the other parent?

- Do you try your best to keep money issues as a private, adult matter separate from your children?

- Do you ask your children about your former spouse's "new friends"?

- Do you arbitrarily change visitation plans on your former spouse as a means of controlling him or her?

- Have you maintained rather consistent schedules, chores, and the same type of discipline since the divorce?

- Can you listen to your child tell you about how they spent their time with the other parent without reacting emotionally?

I want to give you some straightforward rules to live by that I have found to be helpful when it comes to the delicate area of making good decisions about your children post-divorce so that you and your children can be *better*. Here is the most fundamental yet most challenging rule to remember: **Your children are the byproduct of you and your former spouse; therefore, when you make disparaging comments about your child's other parent, you are negating an aspect of your child.** I assure you, if you seriously keep this in mind as you contemplate commenting on your ex's traits, characteristics, or behavior, you can avoid emotionally harming your children.

No matter what their developmental level, all children have some understanding about where they come from. Perhaps it's just a comment about having "Mommy's blue eyes" or "Daddy's nose" when they are little. But eventually children also come to know that there are traits or abilities that they have received from a parent, for instance, a lovely singing voice, being an avid reader, or having advanced mathematical skill.

So what happens when, in frustration or anger, you negatively label some aspect of your former spouse in front of your children? I'll tell you what happens – you negate an aspect of your child. Think about it this way: when your child is young, they are told about the best possible traits that they inherited from both of their parents – they hear it from grandparents, from your friends, a teacher, etc.

Now, all of a sudden, the not-so-wonderful traits of one parent are being pointed out to them (or they overhear it). What is the impact on the child? They have no internal mechanism at their disposal to filter out the negative traits from the positive ones they have already come to know and believe in over the years. How are they possibly expected to know which traits apply to them and which ones don't?

Therefore, the probable impact is that the child becomes

concerned about the negative traits applying to him or her. As they get older, children can begin to develop anxiety about whether they are "destined" to become like one of their parents in ways that are unappealing, such as the parent with a drinking or anger problem. Way too many children hear "you're just like your father (or mother)", said in an angry, frustrated tone.

Such comments also unconsciously transmit a message to the child that just as they are not responsible for the color of their eyes or how tall they will eventually be, they "can't help" inheriting some of these other qualities – and you don't want a child who grows up to believe they aren't accountable for their own behavior! Don't you want your child to understand that they are free to construct the kind of life they wish to have, that their choices produce consequences, that they are responsible for their life, and that it is not a life predestined by the flaws of their parents?

On the other hand, there is another basic rule to follow: **Don't confuse your children by denying reality.** By this, I mean that if your child comments on your former spouse's behavior or reports a troubling incident which occurred when they were with them, of course you shouldn't jump on the opportunity to use it to trash your ex, but don't deny what you know is likely to be true because it is upsetting to you to acknowledge it. This is one of the difficult parts of parenting that causes my divorced patients to ask for help, and it will require some sensitivity and creativity at times on your part.

If your former spouse has a temper and your child comments on Mom or Dad yelling a lot or becoming easily angered, acknowledge this in a neutral way – you and your child know the truth, so don't make it worse but don't deny it. Likewise, if your child complains that they were late for an important event and it was your former spouse's fault because they didn't leave on time and you are well aware that the other parent has a chronic problem with punctuality, acknowledge it and attempt to help your child to find a way to manage such situations.

For example, lets say that your child is visiting with you on the weekend and begins to complain about "Mommy's boyfriends" and tells you that your former wife seems to be dating a lot of guys and is apparently keeping this no secret from your child. You could ignore it in a well-meaning effort not to say anything derogatory about your ex-wife, but that wouldn't address the fact that your child brought the issue up to you in the first place. You could say what you *really* think and use some vulgar terms to describe how you truly feel about your ex-wife's behavior. That would certainly be tempting but would also clearly be violating the first rule I gave you and would ultimately be damaging to your child.

This is a challenging moment to choose your words very carefully while not denying the reality of what your child has been observing. It's very difficult to balance privacy with honesty. You could respond with something along the lines of "you know, your Mom is very sociable and has always liked to go out a lot, so I'm not really surprised. Is there something about Mom having boyfriends that you'd like to talk about?"

This kind of answer lets your child know that you heard them, you've acknowledged some characteristic or behavior of their other parent without negatively labeling it, and you've let them know its okay to talk about it. Obviously, if its something you have a significant concern about, you will need to address it directly and privately with your former spouse.

The next rule is **Encourage a realistic view of how**

your child's life is affected by divorce. Of course your divorce will involve making some changes that will affect your children, but don't make things out to be worse than they really are. Don't forget that an important part of your role as a parent is that you are always preparing your children for change because change will be an inevitable part of their future when they are adults. It is always preferable if you can keep major changes to a minimum in the midst of or following a divorce, but sometimes it is simply not possible.

You may be feeling angry, scared and uncertain about the future, but don't subject your child to unpleasant, possibly self-fulfilling prophecies. You probably didn't share your personal, innermost worries with your child prior to getting a divorce (at least I certainly hope you didn't), so why would you do so now? If you didn't divulge detailed financial concerns prior to your divorce, don't start doing it now.

It is certainly appropriate to explain to your child that you must move to a different house or apartment, but balance the explanation of what is factually happening with only a small dose of the details about *why* and emphasize the potential advantages to the change. For example, it's okay to tell your child that you are selling your car and buying a different one because you think it is a good financial decision. Its *not* okay to include your child in a discussion about how you'll probably have to drive some inferior car compared to the one you had before and how you don't have enough money for gas because your ex-husband isn't paying enough child support.

Your child may have to attend a different school as a result of some decisions made following your divorce. Don't apologize repeatedly for this or predict future failure.

Don't doom your child if they must make the transition from a private to a public school by telling them how inferior their education is going to be.

Help your child to see the opportunity in the obstacle – find out about the school and enthusiastically share the information with your child and support them in making new friends. In other words, anticipate the possible benefits that may come about as a result of changing schools. The ability to perceive good aspects of change is an important skill to impart to your child.

Likewise, please don't make promises you can't keep. Don't try to make the divorce somehow more palatable by providing your child with some fantasy that you can't deliver. Don't promise expensive gifts that you wouldn't otherwise consider buying if you hadn't gone through a divorce just because you now have twinges of guilt.

I've witnessed the noncustodial parent who has to relocate for job purposes promise their children frequent trips to DisneyWorld just because he was moving to take a new job in Florida. That's unreasonable and will eventually disappoint the child and affect the child's trust in their parent. If you didn't take your child to an amusement park every other weekend when you were married, why would you be promising that now simply because you are divorced?

If you are the one who left the home and doesn't reside with your child full-time, don't promise your child that they can come and spend the entire summer with you when you know that isn't part of your divorce agreement. It's guaranteed that either you or your former spouse is going to look like the *bad guy* when summer rolls around and you can't deliver.

Let your child be a child – don't expect them to be a replacement for an adult partner. The custodial parent typically has greater opportunities to slowly have their child's role evolve into that of counselor or confidante simply by virtue of the time spent together. Despite what has happened to your adult relationship with your child's other parent, your child needs to be able to remain at his or her own developmental level. I cringe when I hear a divorced mother refer to her little boy as "my little man" or "the new man of the house".

Please be aware of the insidious and unconscious pressure to overburden your child with adult responsibilities. Don't think that because your child appears "mature" that he or she is ready to take on excessive responsibilities or that it is okay to involve them in your social activities and conversations as if they were an adult.

It is easier to slip into discussing adult matters with your child if you don't have enough opportunities for mature discussions with other adults, so make sure you've got those resources in place. Encouraging your child to contribute to the household by teaching them to take out the trash is one thing; sharing the woes of paying the bills is entirely another. At times when you think you may have crossed that line and placed your child in an adult role, it might be helpful to ask yourself "would I be doing or saying this if I weren't divorced?"

And finally, **design an atmosphere of consistency.** When life seems chaotic, people tend to need and gravitate more toward consistency. When we are confused or anxious, we seek out stability and comforting rituals. It appears that children need this even more so than adults. Your child needs to have a *reasonable* idea about what is going to happen on any given day.

Don't expect your children to handle this for themselves just because you are preoccupied with the many changes you are experiencing as a result of your divorce. Children are not usually able to impose the necessary structure on their lives by themselves – they need their parents to do it for them.

For example, left to their own devices, most younger children would not go to bed at a reasonable time that is good for their growing bodies and that lets them get enough rest in order to perform well at school or in an athletic activity the next day. Don't let the structure of things such as bedtimes, doing homework, or permitted television shows just go by the wayside because you are feeling overwhelmed by the details of various aspects of your divorce. Consistency creates security, and the lack of consistency or unpredictability is upsetting to children (and to most adults!)

Even in the midst of change, you can develop schedules that will be comforting for everyone. For example, you may be a woman who has returned to full-time employment now that you are divorced, and consequently your schedule has changed. Your children need to know how they will be impacted by this change, so develop a new ritual.

If your child was previously used to having you available immediately after school in the afternoon to help with homework, explain what the new plan will be. For instance, you could emphasize to your child that you are still just as interested in how their day was and what's going on in school, but that with the change in your schedule, you'll be reviewing their homework and helping them right after dinner. Anticipating the impact of the changes in your life and explaining how you will modify the schedule models flexibility and an ability to embrace change – an attitude and behavior that your children can benefit from.

In my experience, I've seen parents allow some weird indulgences to their children that were not ultimately in their children's best interests but were based in the parent's guilt and feeling *sorry* for the children. Your children do not need you to feel sorry for them. They need you to behave like a responsible adult who makes difficult decisions that they should not have to make and are not yet ready to make. Anticipate that there will be changes – and then adapt!

Chapter 7

Your New Healthy Lifestyle

"Nothing is a waste of time if you use the experience wisely."

Rodin

By now, I hope you feel compelled to view the event of divorce in a new way and are ready to begin putting all of the pieces of this puzzle together. You may have already realized that happiness cannot be planned for and arranged, although we frequently act as if it can when we state that this is what we want. Patients often summarize their situation by saying to me "I want to be happy", but the problem arises when you attempt to define exactly what would constitute happiness for that individual.

So things are different now, but by now you are more aware that different doesn't mean worse.

You have probably already noticed that social relationships may abruptly change through a divorce. People you were sure were your friends suddenly stop calling. You likely have lost a friend or acquaintance (or two) simply because those people felt a need to align themselves with your former spouse. I lost some acquaintances in this manner, too. At first I was quite surprised, but over time, it made sense. This is an extremely common phenomenon, and as hurtful as it may seem, you must accept their decision.

You must stop attempting to elicit pity and to convince others that you are an innocent victim of circumstances if you are to be *better*. Your goal is to have friends who are healthy and supportive and who build you up, not friends who are judgmental, critical, tear you down, and who deep down inside really think that your former spouse is better off without you. Don't cling to a friend who needs to leave you simply because you have been through a divorce.

On the other hand, I would caution you to be alert to the friend who seems to be supportive of you but who never misses an opportunity to take a cheap shot at your former spouse or to remind you of some hurtful thing he or she did to you. At first, you may feel like you need to hear those words of validation, but over time such bashing of your ex can serve to reinforce negative feelings that you are working on freeing yourself from.

Being constantly reminded of the past transgressions of your former spouse can unwittingly shift you toward adopting a victim stance. Even though you may have a longstanding friendship, some of your friend's specific behaviors may not be supportive to your growth as a divorced person.

You must be direct but polite and let them know that you are working on making a better life for yourself. This includes learning from the past without dwelling on the past, and so their reminders of painful issues about your former spouse are not helpful at this time. Of course, if they are unwilling or unable to change their behavior, you'll have to take responsibility to change yours – you'll need to spend less time with someone who can't be supportive of the new direction your life is taking.

Consequently, now is also the ideal time to re-evaluate the relationships in your life to determine which ones might actually obstruct you from becoming *better*. This is another way of looking at your investments, because relationships require time, energy and commitment – relationships are an investment.

What do you look for and value in a relationship? Which relationships no longer meet your needs? Its unfortunate but true that some people really do like melodrama and misery and can't genuinely be supportive of someone's happiness.

It's also unfortunate that some people feel that they are entitled to judge or condemn you, to shame you for what you have gone through, or to openly criticize you for being divorced. You can control your exposure to such messages. Don't forget that it is entirely your choice with whom you spend time as well as which individuals you avoid. A real friend is one who will celebrate how you are growing, changing, and finding the opportunities in the obstacle.

It is well-known that people who are surrounded by a network of genuinely supportive friends and relatives generally fare much better in handling any of the multitude of stressors that life throws at us, and it is most certainly true when it comes to divorce.

Take some time to review the interactions you've had with friends and family since your divorce. I'll admit there are some people who thrive on inconsistency, but it's likely that you will see a consistent pattern. It is highly unlikely that someone who is typically appreciative, honest, and supportive will also be demeaning, inattentive, and critical. If you find yourself repeatedly feeling frustrated in a relationship, gingerly trying to explain your position, hoping that they'll understand you, take an honest look at how consistent that person's behavior is. Could it be that they've always been this way and you've kept waiting for them to change or to somehow meet your needs even though that's not their nature?

Be aware of the relationships that exhaust you. How can you identify whether a relationship is simply draining your energy and demanding too much from you? Here's one clue: if you have caller I.D. on your phone, who are the people you avoid talking to or the sight of their name or phone number makes you inwardly cringe? Those are indications of exhausting relationships. Do you have e-mails or phone calls from certain individuals that you avoid, dread returning, or do not return at all? They are exhausting you. You should focus your energy on healing, not on avoiding.

What about the relationship where that individual's behaviors or beliefs somehow put your ethics and morals in conflict? Why do you continue such a relationship? Can you identify some benefit you derive from such a relationship? How many family members or friends do you have an unresolved conflict with that just continues to hang over the relationship like a dark storm cloud?

Let me give you an example from my practice. One of my clients was a middle-aged, single mother who had really been struggling with this issue. Social relationships had never been all that easy for her, but she found herself becoming increasingly avoidant about social interactions with many of her friends. It was unclear at first why she was feeling so uncomfortable with most of her longstanding friends, but what was clear was that the interactions were no longer rewarding and somehow left her feeling worse than if she had just stayed at home.

So we began to try to analyze what happened when she socialized with these people. It quickly became apparent that a major aspect of the problem was that my client had serious financial limitations which her friends blatantly ignored. She would repeatedly be invited to do things which she simply could not afford. In order to maintain the friendships, on more than one occasion she chose to go along with them to expensive restaurants and then would claim to not feel well or not be hungry and would often simply order a cup of tea. Even while in the presence of her so-called "friends", she often felt left out and inferior.

In addition, we identified that these same people tended to ask very pointed, intrusive questions that made her feel uncomfortable and defensive. In contrast, there was another group of friends, two married couples in fact, who were quite wealthy but who were non-judgmental, didn't pry, and who involved my client in appropriate activities where she felt more comfortable and which were more in line with her budget – such as taking their children to the movies and out for ice cream afterwards. When we explored together the different features of these relationships in detail, it became obvious whom she needed to surround herself with and which people she needed to let go of.

Sometimes we need to jettison these difficult and exhausting relationships, but we tend to take the passive route and avoid taking control, waiting for the *other person* to figure it out and let go of *us*. It is easy to become passively frustrating, unavailable, and unresponsive to the other person's needs and silently hope that they will just give up on the relationship first.

But waiting and hoping for this to occur uses up too much of your energy. It's also dishonest and not fair to the other person. Now, at this new stage of your life, is the ideal time to deal with it! Successful people don't wallow in dysfunctional relationships.

Nevertheless, it's usually not a comfortable feeling when you recognize that you have somehow outgrown a friendship. As you focus on creating your new life after divorce you may find it difficult, for example, to work on accepting personal responsibility when a friend is constantly avoiding responsibility by blaming, externalizing and complaining. You may have outgrown the relationship. Making significant changes in your life often provokes unwelcome commentary from friends and family who don't understand exactly what you're going through. The best you can do is to expect it.

On the contrary, though, most of us desire and even feel desperate at times for truly significant, supportive, fulfilling relationships with others. That kind of relationship doesn't blossom from simply tolerating one another but grows instead from a deep sense of community and common values. These are the kind of relationships you want to be pursuing at this point in growing from your divorce experience.

What do you want at this point in your life, as a recently divorced person? You may have figured out by now that I don't believe in luck or coincidences – in fact, most of the people I have treated have heard me say, "there *are* no coincidences." So if it's not about luck, and it's not about chance or coincidence, how do you go about actively constructing this new, healthy, fulfilling lifestyle?

One of the exercises I frequently use with people who have a hard time expressing specifically what they'd like their life to be like (regardless of whether they've been through a divorce), is to ask them to tell me the fantasy version of what they'd like – no holds barred, nothing is out of the question, money is no object kind of fantasizing. Even this is difficult for people who have never genuinely considered taking active control of *constructing* their own life through their own choices.

I usually have to prod people a bit, such as asking them about the places in the world they've always dreamed of visiting. I also ask them what they used to think they'd be when they "grew up". What else might they have pursued? What kind of work would they do if the compensation were not an issue? How would their life be if they could magically make it different *today*?

What small, private thing could they do to nurture themselves even if others might think it silly? It's amazing what we can hold ourselves back from just because of the notion that someone might not approve or might think it frivolous. It's okay to be bold – even outrageous! You can engage in this same exercise with yourself. Once you become aware of some of those ideas, it's easier to develop a plan for whether you can get there and how you are going to get there.

You may be asking yourself, how will you know that you're no longer bitter, that those ugly feelings are finally gone? How will you know that you've healed sufficiently emotionally and are truly becoming *better*?

It is different for every individual, but if you have taken responsibility and worked on forgiving yourself for what transpired in the marriage as well as forgiving your former spouse, you've achieved a level of freedom that allows you to truly build a new life. It all boils down to how *you* decide the outcome of your divorce will be and if you are willing to simply settle. Don't demand anything less than the absolute best from yourself. Some of you may still be questioning whether the outcome is totally up to you – I assure you that *it is.* You may never get an opportunity like this again!

When people begin to spontaneously comment on the positive changes they observe in you, this is feedback that lets you know you are healing. When you find yourself approaching a new day with excitement about the unknown instead of worry and dread, you will know that you are healing. When you accept an invitation to try something new instead of automatically saying no, that's movement in the direction of healing.

When you find yourself making it a priority to take care of *you,* you are healing. Are you committed to caring for yourself so that you may better care for those who are dependent upon you? When you no longer cling to the notion that you are a victim of circumstances, you will know that you are healing. If you are aware of feeling even a glimmer of enthusiasm about the possibilities for your future right now as you are nearing the end of this book, that's an indication that you are viewing your divorce through healthier eyes and are healing.

Are you at least moving in the right direction somewhere on the path of knowing what your values truly are? What have you learned the real priorities are in your life through the experience of your divorce? Have you allowed the experience of your divorce to clarify those issues on which you cannot compromise?

Are you clearer on how you will define your character in comparison to how it was prior to your divorce? I certainly hope that you are. You don't have to be living it all yet, just moving in the direction of the person you know you want to be.

Have you decided what spiritual practice makes sense for you? How and where will you practice your faith?

With whom will you share your spirituality?

To what extent have you renegotiated all of your relationships as a single, divorced person? Are you still expecting the worst? Are you ready and willing to let go of relationships that don't work? Are you still hoping that someone else will make you happy? Are you willing to acknowledge your self-destructive habits? Are you waiting to somehow be proven right? There's nothing to prove here, so just focus on being right with yourself. Peacefully accepting that some relationships must end, some of your relationships must change and be redefined, and that new relationships must be openly embraced is evidence that you are healing.

As a result of being faced with a crisis and being challenged to look for the opportunity in the obstacle, do you feel like you are approaching this new stage of your life from a point of strength or weakness? If you have made a conscious decision to be *better,* you are starting from a position of strength. Is it possible that you'll experience setbacks? Of course it is – expect them and then actively deal with them.

Being strong means that you are actively working on strategies to develop a healthy lifestyle – you are not waiting for it to happen to you. Do you feel like you are actively contributing to the world?

Don't be surprised if you find yourself with an opportunity in the near future to offer support and encouragement to someone else who is going through a divorce. If you consciously choose to use what is presented in this book to create a *better* life, you will be prepared to be a blessing to others, and you will know that you are contributing to the world.

In fact, your transformation and visibly improved life will actually draw others to you who are experiencing what you've experienced in order to find out the secret of your peace, contentment, and progress. Lend them your ear, your optimism, and this book.

Always remember, your life isn't about where you start; it's about where you finish. *Choose* to finish *better*.

Help Is But A Click Away -

A MESSAGE FROM THE PUBLISHER

In my troubled youth, I discovered the hope and knowledge available in self-help books. I subsequently became a psychologist and went on to write five self-help books. I was so impressed by the power of self-help books that when the Internet became so prevalent in our lives, I realized it was the ideal place for people to find help. *SelfHelpBooks.com* emerged and is readily available to anyone who is in need of help.

SelfHelpBooks.com publishes books by mental health professionals as well as by lay people who have coped with life's adversity and have valuable advice to pass on to the rest of us. The titles that can be found in *SelfHelpBooks.com*'s virtual bookstore have been carefully selected to provide help for a range of problems from addiction to depression, from fear to loneliness, and from problems of youth to problems of the elderly.

At *SelfHelpBooks.com* we think we have a book for almost every problem. If you need help immediately, you can download it as an E book. If you are in less of a hurry, you can order a print version and receive it within days.

If you visit SelfHelpBooks.com and don't find a book relating to your particular problem, contact us and we will immediately add books in that category. If you know of a particular self-help book that has helped you, let us know and we will add it to our list as well.

Harold H. Dawley, Jr., Ph.D., ABPP
Publisher

Printed in the United States
58141LVS00004B/73

9 781587 411106